RAPE 101

RAPE 101

Sexual Assault Prevention
For College Athletes

by Andrea Parrot, Nina Cummings
and Timothy Marchell

LP **LEARNING PUBLICATIONS, INC.**
Holmes Beach, Florida

ISBN 1-55691-099-1

Learning Publications, Inc.
5351 Gulf Drive
P.O. Box 1338
Holmes Beach, FL 34218-1338

Printing: 5 4 3 2 1   Year: 8 7 6 5 4

Printed in the United States of America.

CONTENTS

FOREWORD

During the summer of 1990, prior to my first season as the Head Football Coach at Cornell University, Dr. Andrea Parrot approached me with a unique idea. Her proposal was to present a program on date rape education to our entire football team; a group that consisted of approximately 120 student-athletes.

Never before had an intercollegiate team of this size at Cornell taken on a voluntary educational program dealing with this social issue. My initial thought was "Why should we?" No member of our team had been involved in a charge of date or gang rape. Why should we subject our team members to the potential criticism and cynicism that could erupt from people outside our program when they learned of our involvement in this proactive presentation?

Simply, it made sense. For years, intercollegiate athletic programs, with coordination through their sports medicine and student health services departments, have been conducting preventative programs on alcohol and drug use. Tremendous amounts of time and money have been spent educating student athletes on the effects of the alleged performance-enhancing anabolic steroids. We have not, however, had alcohol or drug problems with our players and we have shown a 100% success rate (180/180 negative test results) on our 5 NCAA sanctioned mandatory steroid urinalysis tests since the commencement of testing in the fall of 1990. To educate our players on the phenomenon of date rape and gang rape is simply a continuation of the off-the-field and outside-the-classroom learning process we have created on the previously mentioned subjects.

We are committed to creating an environment where our student athletes can develop a positive self-image. When that occurs, it is more likely that they will be able to show that same respect to their peers, and lead a healthy and happy life here at Cornell.

Jim Hofher
Head Football Coach
Cornell University 1994

PREFACE

This manual represents our collective wisdom about conducting sexual assault prevention programs for male college athletes. Because we were traveling uncharted waters in our work with Cornell University student athletes, we had to base our initial strategies on both educational theory and our experience leading sexual assault prevention programs for other groups. Some of our attempts worked well, and others did not. Given the lack of guidelines for working with this population, there is certainly much more to be learned. However, we feel that the energy of others should be spent innovating rather than reinventing the wheel we have already crafted. Therefore, we offer this manual as a foundation on which to build. It offers suggestions on how to work with coaches as well as athletes, and provides both theoretical information and practical advice.

Social change is a slow process, and is likely to take many interventions in order to make a serious impact. We have taken that fact into consideration in the planning and execution of our programs at Cornell. Furthermore, we have had to engage in some philosophical compromise and you may notice those compromises reflected in this manual. We believe that certain political positions are important when it comes to rape education, but so is being effective. It is possible that if you are successful in getting the athletic department to allow you to speak to the athletes about rape prevention, that this may well be the student-athlete's first exposure to the issue. It is crucial that we not discourage the athletes from hearing the message by using too strong political rhetoric. If you can get the athletes to hear your message during an initial program, they may be willing to attend other programs on sexual assault prevention in the future.

We believe that all high risk groups of men should be targeted for rape prevention efforts. Considerable work has already been done on educating other high risk groups, such as fraternity men (with video programs such as "Playing The Game," which is sponsored in part by Delta Tau Delta, Phi Gamma Delta, and Sigma Nu), but no comprehensive written guide has been available for working with athletes. We hope this will be the first of many such resources. It is our hope that this manual will enable you to effectively educate male athletes and thereby help stem the tide of sexual assault on college campuses.

The Cornell Program

In 1990, Cornell's varsity football coach James Hofher accepted our offer to conduct a rape awareness program for his players. The program was proactive in that we did not develop the program in response to a sexual assault charge against a team member. That program's success soon led to requests for presentations from other teams. Because we were invited back annually to meet with the football team, we subsequently developed a four year cycle of sequential programs that could be offered to any team on campus.

As a direct result of the first educational program conducted in 1990, the Cornell varsity football team donated money collected during an athletic fundraiser to the local rape crisis organization. The program had raised the team's awareness of the problem and drawn their attention to the effects of sexual assault on a victim. It motivated the men to do something that would contribute to helping victims. This spontaneous outcome was a welcomed sign of the team's raised awareness of the issue. Rather than silence, the football players did something that, in one small way, showed responsibility for the problem.

How to Use this Manual

It is important to remember that this manual was developed through work with men who do not represent the demographic backgrounds of the average college athlete. They are Ivy League, primarily caucasian, upper middle to upper class athletes from a fairly large school (12,000 undergraduates). None receive athletic scholarships. Their response to sexual assault education may be different than those who play for Big Ten teams or athletes from very small schools.

This manual is not intended to be perfect for every group or team, because each group is different. We have had many successes and some failures, and we have learned from our mistakes. Although these activities may not work for every group exactly as printed, they are likely to be successful if modified according to the needs of your group. The activities were designed to fit into a four year sequence so that they build upon each other year after year. Assuming educators have an opportunity to work with a team annually, the activities will provide a framework that offers interesting and informative opportunities for discussion. The four year sequence is important to remember when selecting activities from the appendices, because some may require that the athletes have been given previous information in order for the activity to work most effectively.

In large schools, it is usually not possible to introduce programs for every team on a college campus in one year and still maintain high quality. Usually, there are not enough staff or students to provide the series of programs that would be most effective. Therefore, the best suggested approach is to find one (or a few) *supportive* coach(es) and talk to him/them about doing such a program. Once they have been "sold" on the value of a presentation, and you have had a successful track record with that team, you will have a coach and the athletes on his team to help you sell the idea to more teams. It is better to start small and develop a good strong foundation than to try to reach every athlete at once. The consequences of trying to educate too many teams at once may be a sloppy job, or even worse, turning people off to the concept and your efforts. A bad program can be worse than no program.

Overview of the Manual

Chapters 1 through *3* provide the theoretical underpinning that guided our efforts when we began developing programs for athletes. *Chapters 1* and *2* offer background on the reasons we have chosen to target athletes. The information may be helpful when educators encounter defensive or resistant administrators. *Chapter 3* outlines several psychosocial factors to consider when working with college athletes and describes some of the dynamics that may be encountered when doing programs with a team.

Chapter 4 details the different approaches that have proved successful for us. Chapters 5 and 6 offer detailed instructions for planning and conducting programs. Finally, Chapter 7 describes the activities that can be used (with adjustments or revisions) for any program with athletes.

ACKNOWLEDGEMENTS

This manual was written to aid the fight against sexual assault. Many people contributed to its development. The authors would like to thank: Alan Berkowitz, Ron Campbell, Sandy Caron, Lettie Caswell, Ishmael Conway, Charles B. Estey III, Robert Heasley, Jim Hofher, Tom Jackson, Jackson Katz, Mary and Dave Maley, Therese & Tom Marchell, The Cornell Varsity Football Team (1990-1993), Beth Van Duyne, and Christopher Wallach.

EDUCATION AS PREVENTION

Rape is a sexual crime, an abuse of power which always involves some use or threat of force. In some cases, men who rape are sexual psychopaths, driven by sadistic urges or hatred of women. These men premeditate rape. However, rape is often an impulsive and opportunistic act committed by "average" individuals. Their initial goal is sexual activity, usually sexual intercourse, and they turn to rape to achieve their goal and the gratification of having power over another person. This dynamic is characteristic of many date rapes.

Cross cultural research shows that rape is virtually absent from certain societies, whereas it is rampant, even ritualized, in others. The difference between these populations is the degree to which societal norms and practices condone or forbid sexual violence and whether the social ideology supports male dominance (Sanday, 1981). In other words, rape is a learned behavior.

North American society, among others, condones such sexual violence and harassment in subtle as well as overt ways. Through sexist jokes, pornography, demeaning media images of women, and court decisions that acquit accused rapists, some men have come to believe that they have a right to sex and that there will be no negative consequence if they obtain it by force. By degrading women and fostering a sense of male entitlement to sex, our culture teaches men that sexual violence is acceptable.

Since rape is, to a large extent, a learned phenomenon, education can play a vital role in preventing it. Rape education for men functions in two basic ways. One is to educate the individual directly, and the other is to reshape the collective attitude of the group to which he belongs. The group's opinion in turn affects the individual. Through this process education plants the seeds for reshaping our culture.

We believe that in all cases, the responsibility for rape lies solely with the perpetrator. Research indicates that certain circumstances can increase the risk of acquaintance rape or sexual assault. Insensitivity to others' feelings, ambiguous sexual norms, differing personal expectations, alcohol use, and peer pressure can interact and contribute to sexual assault. These are some of the factors which rape education can work to change at both the emotional and cognitive level. Yet the pragmatic question remains,

CHAPTER 1

where should we target our efforts? We believe that one among several areas that deserve our attention are *male athletes*.

WHY MALE ATHLETES?

The first and simplest reason for targeting male athletes is that campus rape prevention programs historically have not directed activities at men, whether athletes or not, despite the fact that it is men who rape. Programs traditionally have focused on changing women's behavior rather than men's. But there are distinct advantages to targeting male athletes:

1) Male athletes are a "ready-made" audience. They know each other, depend on one another, and understand how to function as a unit. Because of their reliance on each other, they make good candidates for learning how to exert positive peer pressure. Since there is a natural hierarchy in many team sports, older students, team captains, and star players can be effective informal peer educators. Younger athletes can learn about college life and the reality of an athlete's world from their older peers.

2) The team's coach is a defined leader and potential role model. Coaches often are highly respected by players and have the power to model appropriate attitudes and behaviors. Coaches can set limits to behavior on, as well as off, the playing "field." Coaches also have the authority to require a team to attend educational programs.

3) Athletes are high-profile individuals and often have natural leadership ability. Because they are popular, athletes can play a key role in establishing standards for acceptable behavior in a college community. By participating in rape prevention programs and modeling appropriate behaviors, athletes can send a strong message to other students.

In addition to these practical reasons for working with athletes, this group should be targeted because they appear to be at higher risk for committing sexual assaults. Athletes face a unique constellation of factors which interact to foster attitudes and social situations that increase the likelihood of sexual assault. For those athletes trained to be violent, the risk of committing sexual assault increases if they carry their aggression into relationships "off the field." Depending on which sport is involved, other factors can include: a sense of impunity resulting from high status, having to interpret sexually ambiguous attention from female fans, high levels of alcohol or drug use, and the peer pressure that accompanies involvement in all-male groups. In 1994 many of these factors were associated with the highly publicized arrest of O.J. Simpson for the alleged murder of his former wife. They are not only factors which lead to sexual assault, they also may lead to battering and even more severe types of violence.

We have found that many coaches and athletes share our motivation for offering sexual assault education. These men have daughters, sisters, and friends whom they care about, and they want to prevent violence against them. Furthermore, no athlete wants his or a teammates's career, education, and life jeopardized by a sexual assault charge. Nor do coaches want to lose star athletes. Moreover, the positive publicity and team morale generated by a prevention program is far more desirable than damaging media coverage resulting from an arrest.

Legal Requirements

There is increasing legislative pressure on colleges to provide comprehensive sexual assault education, including programs for athletes. Since September 1, 1991, the Federal "Student Right to Know Act" has required colleges and universities to collect data on campus crime, including rape. Under Title II of the Campus Awareness and Crime Security Act, each school is required to publish these crime statistics annually so that students and their families can make informed judgements about campus safety. Colleges are required to make information available to students and employees about campus security policies at least once a year. A school with a policy of extensive sexual assault education demonstrates a commitment to student safety. For example, Forbes Magazine's 1991 Best Schools issue highlighted Cornell's rape prevention program as evidence of the university's concern for student welfare.

As of 1993, four states (CA, NY, WI, MN) have passed legislation relating to sexual assault education, prevention, policies, and reporting on college campuses. In addition, the Chancellor of the Florida State Universities has required his schools to conduct acquaintance rape education programs. California has the most comprehensive legislative mandate, which requires that among the groups to receive sexual assault information, athletic teams specifically should be targeted.

As mentioned previously, traditionally most campuses initiated acquaintance rape prevention based on stranger rape prevention strategies (such as locking doors, not walking alone, and improving lighting on campus). While important safety measures, these methods usually are not effective in preventing acquaintance rapes. While stranger rapists start out with the intent to rape a woman, acquaintance rapists are frequently men whose intent is to be sexual with someone they know, i.e., a date, friend, or colleague. The sexual goal becomes rape once any degree of resistance is encountered. Therefore, prevention programs must inform men about acceptable forms of sexual interaction and then clearly identify the elements of sexual assault (Parrot, et al., 1994).

ATHLETES AS PERPETRATORS: CASES AND EVIDENCE

Rape is a nationwide problem not limited to athletes. Over 20% of college women report being the victim of a rape or attempted rape before graduating (Koss, et al., 1987). Certainly not all of these rapes and attempted rapes are committed by athletes, and likewise most athletes are not rapists. Yet sexual abuse by athletes can be found at every level from high school to the professional teams. In 1990 more than fifty athletes were involved in reported sexual assault cases nationwide (Eskanazi, 1991). Although it is not exactly clear what percentage of perpetrators are athletes, there are data and abundant anecdotes to suggest that athletes may commit sexual assaults at a higher rate than non-athletes.

Several cases have focused national attention on sexual assault by high school athletes. In 1993, three high school football players from Glen Ridge, New Jersey, were convicted of aggravated sexual assault of a developmentally disabled teenage girl. In Sunnyside, Washington, a high school wrestler was anally gang raped with a broom handle by his own teammates. The "Spur Posse," a group of high school athletes in Lakewood, CA, made headlines amid charges of sexual conquests which included assaults on girls as young as eleven-years-old.

Despite the publicity generated by these cases, sexual assault, especially gang rape, occurs more often at the hands of college athletes. While peer pressure, alcohol and drug use, and involvement in all male groups contribute to the likelihood of an acquaintance rape by a single assailant, they are crucial elements in the commission of a gang rape. The male bonding present within teams has been found to contribute to gang rape. In addition, most gang rape charges against athletes involve members of contact sports such as football and basketball, rather than athletes of individual sports such as tennis or golf (Sandler, as cited in Neimark, 1991; Rosen, 1993).

The charges of sexual assault by athletes also extends into the pros. In the last decade many famous cases of sexual assault involving college and professional athletes have received national media attention.

CHAPTER 2

College

- University of Colorado — 2 football players were charged with rape, acquitted, and left school.

- University of Florida — a defensive tackle was arrested and charged with sexual battery for holding a student at knife point.

- University of Minnesota — three basketball players were charged with committing a gang rape after a game in Madison, Wisconsin.

- St. John's University in Queens — a woman claimed to have been sexually assaulted by five members of the lacrosse team.

- University of California, Berkeley — a first year student claimed to have been gang raped by four football team members.

- Syracuse University — a football player, Tom Watson was charged with criminal counts of rape and sodomy. He pled guilty to sexual misconduct.

- University of Oklahoma — Nigel Clay, a football player, is serving ten years in prison for acquaintance rape.

Professional:

- Mike Tyson — former heavyweight boxing champion was convicted of raping and sodomizing a contestant for the Black Miss America Pageant. He was sentenced to six years in jail.

- Gerald Perry — All-pro Denver Broncos football player was charged with and acquitted of rape but agreed to counseling.

- Aaron Pryor — former Junior Welter Weight Champion was charged with committing a sexual assault and pled no contest to a lesser charge.

- Kevin Allen — Philadelphia Eagles football team lineman was found guilty of rape and was sentenced to three years in prison.

- Mossy Cade — Green Bay Packers football player was convicted of rape.

The NFL's Cincinnati Bengals — in 1992 10 former and current team members were named in a civil suit for participating in a gang rape in 1990, and 10 others were named for observing the rape.

Four members of the Washington Capitols hockey team were accused of sexually assaulting a 17 year old woman. The players were cleared of the charges, although a teammate reportedly told investigators that he had seen the athletes wrestling with the woman.

Lisa Olsen, sports reporter for the Boston Herald, was sitting in the New England Patriots locker room interviewing a player when several naked team members positioned their genitals near her face and made lewd suggestions to her. The club and three of the Patriots were ordered to pay $72,500 in fines.

"It was swept under the rug. If you didn't know anything about it from the inside, you weren't going to hear anything about it from the outside."

In addition to the above cases, reports from counselors, former victims, and athletes suggest that there are many assaults by athletes, particularly college athletes, which are never reported. A 1990 *New York Times* article quoted Marybeth Roden of the Rape Treatment Center at Santa Monica Hospital: "I'd say a significant number of our clients have been gang raped by athletes." From prison, while serving time for a drug conviction, former University of Oklahoma star Charles Thompson told a television talk-show host about a gang rape by 12 athletes that was never reported: "It was swept under the rug. If you didn't know anything about it from the inside, you weren't going to hear anything about it from the outside."

Studies

Beyond individual cases, there is a growing body of data linking college athletes to sexual assault. For example:

A 1986 survey of some 200 college police departments and rape counselors by the Philadelphia Daily News found that athletes were reported for raping a student once every 18 days on average and that they were nearly 40 percent more likely to be reported for rape than other males on campus (Hoffman, 1986).

A study of 24 gang sexual assault at colleges found that most involved fraternity brothers or members of athletic teams, primarily football and basketball squads (O'Sullivan, 1991).

CRITICISM

While some studies have shown that the incidence of rape among athletes appears to be higher than among the general student population, there has not been a comprehensive study to measure the frequency of rape by athletes. Still, leaders in the field of sexual assault prevention feel there is enough evidence to support the idea, especially in the instance of gang rape.

The rape prevention programs targeting male athletes do have their critics, who argue that the majority of athletes do not rape, and that most rapists are not athletes. They contend that other forces — such as family and the media — are the primary factors involved. Nevertheless, peer influence also powerfully shapes beliefs and actions. Young men may teach each other a narrow definition of masculinity which they learn from our sports culture: being tough, dominating, and stoic. These qualities may increase the risk of committing a sexual assault.

ATHLETIC CULTURE
AND SEXUAL VIOLENCE

Athletes are socialized in special ways in our culture. Famous athletes are admired and respected as "superhuman," and because of their celebrity status they can sell anything from aftershave to underwear. Their high status and fame tend to support feelings of impunity and the belief that they are above the law, or that laws don't apply to them. They are trained to be aggressive on the field, court, or ice, and many of them don't know when or how to turn the aggression off after the game. They also may not know how to interpret the signals of female "fans" who "throw" themselves at them after a game. Peer pressure is often also involved in convincing a reluctant athlete to participate in an assault [as is often the case in a gang rape situation] (Parrot, Cummings, Marchell & Hofher, 1994). "In *The Hundred Yard Lie,* Rick Telander, a reporter for *Sports Illustrated,* writes that he has heard so much degrading talk of women in the locker room he's sure that the macho attitudes promoted by coaches contribute [perhaps unwittingly] to the athlete's problems in relating to women" (Nelson, 1994, p. A21).

SPORTS AND MASCULINITY

Male socialization patterns combined with athletic training can be a volatile mixture. As a part of masculinity development, male athletes are exposed to a socialization backdrop in which males are:

- less likely to be held;

- more likely to be hit by parents;

- more likely to experience parental/family/peer pressure to be aggressive;

- less likely to receive loving attention when hurt or injured;

- more likely to be hit/hurt physically by peers as well as teachers, parents, coaches, etc.;

- will be punished more severely than females for not conforming to sex-role expectations.

CHAPTER 3

Additionally, males are simply not given useful information about sex or sexuality. Instead, men are generally informed by similarly naive peers or pornography. Some of the messages they get are:

- masturbation is viewed as second-best or juvenile;

- sex is bad/dirty;

- sex requires manipulation of another person;

- "scoring" wins points with peers;

- sex is not something you discuss with women.

"Timothy Jon Curry, an Ohio State sociologist who employed researchers to record locker-room conversations over several months, found that talk of women as objects took the form of loud performances for other men. Talk about ongoing relationships with women, on the other hand, took place only in hushed tones, often behind rows of lockers, and was subject to ridicule. 'This ridicule tells the athlete that he is getting too close to femaleness, because he is taking relatedness seriously,' he writes. 'Real men do not do that' " (Nelson, 1994, p. A21).

Males seldom, if ever, have role models with whom they can discuss honestly their own sexual feelings or experiences. Thus, young men buy into the stereotypes that are falsely perpetuated in our culture, such as all men are sexually active, or intercourse is the only way to have "real sex." Sensuality remains within the female realm, while men tend to deny their own sensuality. As a result, men look to women for tenderness but treat their own bodies harshly when it comes to sexual activity (good examples are the many terms for masturbation such as "beating off" or "pounding one's meat" which reflect an absence of sensual self-awareness). This lack of self-awareness leads to males being so goal-oriented that "getting some" and "getting off" is the most desirable, but tender sexual activity is perceived as not even possible or desirable (Heasley & Barker, 1994).

While athletic opponents are intended to be adversaries, problems arise when men also view sexual relationships as adversarial: the man's job is to "score," while the woman's job is to be defensive and keep him from "scoring." In general, men who ascribe to traditional sex roles and male sexual dominance are more likely than other men to engage in verbal sexual coercion and forcible rape (Mulehenhard & Falcon, 1990). The extent to which athletes ascribe to these beliefs varies. However, if they tend to do so they are more likely to consider sexual assault acceptable.

Aggression and Sex

"When quarterback Timm Rosenbach of the Phoenix Cardinals quit pro football after the 1992 season, he told Ira Berkow of the *New York Times:* 'I though I was turning into some kind of animal. You go through a week getting yourself up for a game by hating the other team, the other players. You're so mean and hateful, you want to kill somebody. Football's so aggressive. Things get done by force. And they you come home, you're supposed to turn it off? Oh, here's your lovin' daddy. It's not that easy. It was like I was an idiot. I felt programmed. I had become a machine' " (Nelson, 1994, p. A21).

Controlled aggression is an important part of many contact sports. However, the adrenalin rush of physical competition may be carried over to post game activities. This sensation may mediate the man's guilt and self-doubt in a sexually charged situation (Gondolf, as cited in Neimark, 1991). Thus, an athlete may take what he wants in an aggressive way off the field in much the same manner as he did on the field (Neimark, 1991). In this mindset aggression may merge with sexuality and lead to a sexual assault.

Members of aggressive team sports, particularly football and basketball, are charged with rape more frequently than athletes from non-contact sports such as baseball or swimming (*Time,* 1990). Controlled aggression is a normal part of these contact sports and on the field there are clearly understood rules which limit aggression, with officials present to enforce them (although sometimes athletes are encouraged to get away with as much as they can regardless of the rules). However, the same is not true with sexual relationships. Men and women are rarely taught any "rules" about sexual behavior and there is certainly no one "officiating" their actions (Marchell, et al., 1992) Moreover, men and women are socialized to play the "game" of sex by different rules. Men often compare sex with sports by the terms they use to describe it:

"How far did you get?"

"We got to second base last night, but the next time we go out I think I'll score."

Athletic training may have other implications for the way a man communicates in a sexual encounter. For example, some skills which enable an athlete to dominate his opponent involve deception. What might be considered "lying" in a social setting is a perfectly legitimate strategy to accomplish the goal of winning a football game. Elgin (1993) describes it this way:

"It's really a sense of power that comes from specialness, reputation, money — whether it's an athlete, businessman, or entertainer. Anyone who finds himself at the center of the world they're in has a sense of impunity."

"In a football game it's okay to behave as if you have the ball when you don't have it, or vice-versa. It's okay to behave as if you're going to run one direction when you fully intend to run the other. It's okay to set up deceptions in which two or three of the players work together to mislead the other team. None of this is called 'lying' or 'cheating' or 'breaking' a promise." The better a player is at doing these things, the greater the player's value to the team."

Athletic competition may also foster the attitude that the end justifies the means. In sports such as football and hockey, players often bend the rules which regulate violence. It is not unusual for athletes to try to get away with aggression intended to intimidate other players. Miedzian quotes Keith Lee, a former New England Patriots football player: "Nothing's illegal unless you get caught. That's the rule." (Miedzian, 1991). Athletes must be able to make the distinction between what is appropriate as a "game strategy" and what is unethical and immoral "game playing" in life.

Status and Impunity

Athletes' high status and fame may foster the belief that they are above the law, or that laws don't apply to them. Special treatment by fans, schools, alumni, and coaches can foster a sense of entitlement and even exemption from society's normal rules. For example, one college basketball coach phoned a female raped by one of his players, and pressured her to drop charges so she wouldn't hurt the player's reputation and the team's ability to win. Another basketball coach explained to a television reporter, "I think that if rape is inevitable, [she should] relax and enjoy it."

The high social status that may instill a sense of impunity can also increase an athlete's chances of committing a sexual assault. As Hall of Fame hockey goalie Ken Dryden told the *New York Times* in a June 3, 1990 article, "It's really a sense of power that comes from specialness, reputation, money — whether it's an athlete, businessman, or entertainer. Anyone who finds himself at the center of the world they're in has a sense of impunity."

Impunity for athletes who rape is not unusual. For example, in 1986, Syracuse University football player Tom Watson was accused by a first-year student of rape and was convicted in criminal court of sexual misconduct. He was sentenced to three years probation and 300 hours of community service, but the University's judicial board came to his assistance and ruled that he had not violated school policy. Watson stayed in school, kept his scholarship, and continued to play football. Only later did the school's chancellor suspend him from the team — for five games.

From prison, convicted rapist Nigel Clay, an ex-University of Oklahoma football player, explained to a talk-show host how this sense of impunity fosters rape: "You seem like you're protected. You can do anything you want, and most athletes, by the time they get into prime-time, feel that they are above the law, that whatever they do, their coach will pull it out . . . or that someone in high power will cover up anything you do."

In contrast, some coaches are leading the way in disciplining players who commit sexual violence. When a University of Tennessee student filed a sexual assault complaint against three of the school's football players during the 1990 season, head Coach Johnny Majors immediately suspended them, and called the incident "an embarrassment to our team, our coaches, and our university." At a press conference called the morning after the alleged incident, Majors explained his stance: "I am taking action today despite a lack of documented information for two reasons: because of the seriousness of the allegations and because there was a clear violation of team rules [the players broke curfew and dorm visitation rules]." Although the woman later decided against pursuing the charge and Majors reinstated the players, such firm action taken immediately sends a strong message to potential abusers (Marchell, et al., 1992).

"You seem like you're protected. You can do anything you want, and most athletes, by the time they get into prime-time, feel that they are above the law, that whatever they do, their coach will pull it out . . . or that someone in high power will cover up anything you do."

GROUP DYNAMICS

Pressure, Conformity and Performance

Researchers report that many rapes, particularly gang rapes, occur in all-male dorms or housing and among men affiliated with some kind of all-male organization (Ehrhart & Sandler, 1985; Warshaw, 1988, O'Sullivan, 1991). In addition to being members of a team, many athletes are members of fraternities. They may be acculturated into an environment that supports traditional male roles, objectification of women, and sexual entitlement; beliefs that have been associated with the likelihood to commit rape (Malamuth, 1981).

"They are raping for each other. The woman is incidental."

"We never talked about respecting women." This man, who later signed with the Philadelphia Eagles, recalls college teammates making crude boasts about sexual conquests. His college teammates hosted "pig parties." The man who brought the ugliest date would win a trophy. This football star says he learned to respect women from his mother and three athletic sisters, and did not attend the parties. But he would laugh at his teammates' jokes, which he now regrets.

"I remember the first time they showed the trophy," in the locker room, he says. "I was a 17-year-old freshman in a room full of upperclassmen. It was boisterous, raunchy, there was screaming and yelling. I laughed along. Men are extremely cliquish. I didn't want to be left out" (Nelson, 1994, p. A21).

Peer pressure contributes to rape because the man, after a date, believes that he is expected to "report" what happened to his friends in the locker room or because other men are there encouraging him to "do it" (as is often the case in a gang rape situation).

The social dynamics of all-male groups, whether they are athletic teams or fraternities, increases the risk of gang rape. In sexually charged situations, intense commitment to a group can impede moral reasoning. "They will do anything to please each other," says psychologist Bernice Sandler. "They are raping for each other. The woman is incidental." Sanday (1990) supports the notion that gang rape situations develop when "group think" takes over and men "perform" for each other. Chris O'Sullivan, who has studied gang rape incidents on campuses, acknowledged that "It usually occurs in a group of young men with a team spirit and usually with those living together. I think they end up relating to each other so intensely even their sexual experiences become shared" (Eskenazi, 1990).

Informal initiation into the campus sports culture begins during recruiting visits by high school athletes. During weekend recruiting trips to the campus, impressionable young men are immersed into the social world of college athletics for the first time. They often are eager to be accepted by the college athletes with whom they are staying. Consequently, they are likely to adopt the social norms they observe during the visit. The risk of sexual assault increases if these norms include anti-social behavior, alcohol abuse or sexual harassment of female students.

Most of the women whom male players see are not coaches or other athletes. They are the short-skirted cheerleaders and the university "hostesses" who escort them around campus during the recruiting process. The locker room is not a place to brag about your wife's or girlfriend's accomplishments. It is a place where men discuss women's bodies in graphic sexual terms, where they boast about "scoring" and joke about beating women (Nelson, 1994, p. A21).

Special Treatment and Sexual Entitlement

As high-status, high-profile students on a college campus, athletes may be accustomed to considerable sexual attention from female fans. Since women often pursue sexual encounters with players, some athletes expect that they can have sex with anyone they want, at any time. This assumption can lead an athlete to misinterpret non-sexual attention from a fan as sexual interest. Athletes may not know how to interpret the signals of female "fans" who "throw" themselves at the athletes after a game. Female fans who express constant adoration for players are at risk for sexual assault because players have difficulty in distinguishing between platonic fans and a willing sexual partner, especially when alcohol or drugs is involved.

In some cases, athletes have been provided with "available" women by well-meaning mentors when they were being recruited by the school. The messages athletes get from these practices contribute to their belief that no women are out of reach and that they can simply take what they want.

The Alcohol Connection

Alcohol can unlock pent-up aggression, dull perceptions, and make oneself more vulnerable to peer pressure. It is undeniably a significant factor in the commission of acquaintance rape and sexual assault, but especially for athletes. According to a UCLA study, college athletes are more likely than non-athletes to consume excessive amounts of alcohol during a single sitting (ACHA, 1992).

Post-game partying contributes to the risk of rape: whether the athletes are celebrating a victory or "drowning their sorrows." After a loss, athletes may drink considerable amounts of alcohol.

Alcohol has traditionally played an important role in the way in which sexual behavior is viewed by both men and women. The double standard has been very important in excusing male behavior regarding sex (i.e., "He got so drunk he didn't know what he was doing," or "He got so drunk he couldn't control himself."). In contrast, women historically have been held accountable for their sexual assault victimization because of their excessive alcohol use (i.e., "She got herself drunk, and passed out, what did she expect?").

Koss, et al., 1987 studied 6,000 American college students and examined their acquaintance rape and sexual assault experiences. A significant incidence of alcohol related sexual victimization was reported. Of those cases reported to the police, 75% of the assailants and 50% of the female victims had been drinking alcohol. This figure may even be low because it excludes all women who "blacked out" from excessive alcohol consumption and do not remember the assault; therefore, they could not report it to the police. It also excludes many victims who fear being charged with underage drinking, or were so drunk that they fear the police will blame them. Many victims blame themselves for getting drunk and putting themselves into such a dangerous situation. Therefore, alcohol (and drugs) are probably involved in many more than 75% of the cases of sexual assaults by acquaintances.

Homophobia

From a very early age, athletes are conditioned by the language of sport. This language has traditionally been filled with insults to both women and gay men. Players report hearing coaches use slurs such as "sissy," "pussy" and "wuss" to motivate and intimidate young male athletes. Miedzian (1991) reports that the insults suggest "that a boy who is not tough enough, who does not live up to the masculine mystique, is really a girl or homosexual." Such attitudes denigrate women and encourage homophobia within teams.

Strict adherence to traditional gender roles may be motivated by, among other things, homophobia. Men who fear being perceived as being gay may be more likely to act out forcefully to prove that they are not. They may have sex with women, willing or unwilling, to prove their heterosexuality. They are more likely to force women to have sex than men who have rejected the more traditional attitudes (Mosher & Anderson, 1986).

Peggy Sanday (1991) argues that homophobia contributes to gang rape. She believes that some homophobic men want to have a close emotional and even sexual relationship with other men. However, they can't imagine actually doing so. Therefore, if they participate in a gang rape they are able to share a sexual experience with other men, without having to have "sex" with them. The victim in the gang rape is simply the vehicle for them to be able to share a sexual experience with each other.

The connection between denigrating women and using homophobia to motivate players may be strong on some teams. Using derogatory terms (calling them "girls," "fags," etc.) to describe players who don't play to their full potential is not unusual. Players may not even recognize the association themselves, but accept the homophobic atmosphere as a part of the motivational message coming from coaches, athletic directors or alumni. One can only imagine how many gay players have had to take part in this type of banter to maintain their privacy and safety on a team.

WORKING WITH COED TEAMS/AUDIENCES

While this manual focuses on sexual assault prevention for male athletes, circumstances may develop in which educators must prepare programs for a mixed audience of male and female teams. The dynamic of the program will change with both men and women present. Many of the activities suggested in this manual are appropriate for mixed audiences and would require only slight variations to make them applicable. Females face some particular issues as athletes and these should be understood when developing programs in which women will be present. The discussion in *Appendix L* outlines some of the special issues for female athletes though these will vary from school to school.

PLANNING A PROGRAM THEORY:
A MORAL DEVELOPMENT APPROACH

The most successful presentations appeal to the life experiences and take into account levels of moral development of the group members. For example, if there has been a member of the team who has been charged and convicted of rape, using that example will make it difficult for them to believe that men are convicted of rape only if they are celebrities, or from another part of the country. Statistics from your community or campus, with examples from their experience (such as mentioning the bars they frequent) will help to personalize the program.

At a typical rape prevention program there will be men at various stages of moral development. William Perry (1970) suggests that college students fall into three basic stages of ethical development: Dualism (right and wrong); Relativism (absolutes may be questioned); and Commitment (ethical view of the rights of others). Kohlberg and Kramer (1969) categorized moral development into Premoral (law and order); Morality of Conventional Role-Conformity (avoiding disapproval of others) and; Morality of Self-Accepted Moral Principles (avoiding self-condemnation). These theories may be applied to help you understand the different moral levels of the students attending your programs.

Many people who fall into the premoral and morality of conventional role conformity categories, and who ascribe to the "Just World Theory," believe that rape victims deserved what they got. If a woman was drunk, many people believe that she deserved to be raped because women shouldn't get drunk. On the other hand, men are often excused for sexual aggression if they have been drinking heavily, because "they can't help themselves." If the woman assaulted has had a bad reputation, whether deserved or not, she is more likely to be blamed for the rape.

THEORETICAL FRAMEWORK
APPLIED TO ATHLETES

To create maximum impact, activities must generate cognitive dissonance by fostering attitudes in the participants which are inconsistent with their behavior. If participants experience sufficient discomfort when faced with the reality of the consequences of rape, they may need to reshape their own sexist attitudes. Educators must persuade men that 1) rape is devastating to the victim, and 2) that attitudes which objectify women contribute to a social climate which fosters rape. Neil Malamuth asked college men anonymously if they would rape if assured of not getting caught, and almost one third of them said yes. These men fall into the Dualism or Premoral stages of moral development. We may be able to create cognitive dissonance for those in the Dualism or Premoral stages by presenting the idea that they may go to jail for having sex with an unwilling partner, and by citing examples with which they can relate (such as Mike Tyson or a local case). Students in the Relativism or Conventional stages may be reached emotionally by asking them how they would feel if someone forced their sisters or girlfriends to have sex against their will. Students at higher levels of moral development probably already believe that sexual assault is always wrong. However, they may not understand how other sexist, objectifying or exploitative behaviors contribute to the incidence of sexual victimization. Those men will benefit from learning that even subtle sexist behaviors contribute to a rape culture mentality.

Appealing to Emotions

In order for any program on a social issue to make an impact, we must address the issues on the affective (feeling) level first, and the cognitive (thinking) level only secondarily. It is unlikely that any man ever stopped forcing sex on women by being told that over 20% of college women experience forced sex during their college years, and that their subsequent interpersonal relationships are almost always troubled as a result of the assault. A man is more likely to reexamine his behavior and reevaluate the importance of satisfying his sexual desires (or his perceived rights) if he can "feel" the anger he would experience if someone close to him, such as a sister or girlfriend, had been raped. Another possible way to help the men "feel" the impact of sexual assault is to help them understand the impact a rape conviction would have on their lives by graphically depicting for them what happens to rapists in prison: they themselves often become rape victims.

The Sexual Violence Progression

The sexual violence progression which follows depicts the relationship between sexual objectification and exploitative behavior and rape. In an attempt to illustrate the cultural and behavioral relationship between misogynistic behaviors contributing to sexual aggression, we developed this graphic. Certainly, there are many more behaviors that are are not shown in the illustration (due to lack of space). The sexual violence progression also begins at a particular point in a continuum of behaviors, ranging from sexist jokes to rape itself.

Sexist Jokes: Becoming desensitized after hearing sexist jokes which are offensive makes it easier for a person to later tell a sexist joke, especially if the person telling the joke is someone held in high esteem. The more the person who is telling the joke is respected, the less offensive the joke is likely to appear. Peer pressure seems to increase the likelihood that men may view inappropriate behaviors as acceptable. For example, when viewing a gang rape scene from the film "The Accused," some audiences of men cheer for the rapists on the screen. For some members of the audience, this cheering may serve to reinforce that gang rape is acceptable behavior.

Sexual Objectification: An attitude in which women are viewed primarily as sexual objects and are denied full respect and dignity. An example of sexual objectification is "scoring" women as they walk by. While talking among themselves, men may comment that a woman is "beautiful, a 10," or she is "a real dog, a 2." This type of objectification escalates to a more serious form if the woman is barked at because she is such a "dog."

There are several factors which both contribute to and are reinforced by sexual objectification. Those factors are: emotional withdrawal, viewing violent pornography, belief that submission is consent, rape fantasies, and sexual harassment.

Emotional Withdrawal: A man who engages in emotional withdrawal is likely to be uninterested in his partners' emotional needs and wishes. He may say "I don't care what you want. What I want is more important."

Viewing violent pornography: There is evidence that this desensitizes people to rape, and is a central element in the socialization of many rapists. A milder form of violence against women may be seen on MTV. More graphic examples of violence against women are seen in "R" rated movies available at video stores for home viewing, such as *I Spit On Your Corpse,* and *Tool Box Massacre.* In one of these films a woman is gang raped, and in the other a naked woman involved in erotic activity is sexually assaulted and then nailed to a wall with a nail gun. Films of this sort reinforce violence against women as acceptable "entertainment."

Belief that Submission is Consent: If a woman stops fighting or saying no, or says nothing, a man may continue to have sex with an unwilling partner.

Rape Fantasies: Men who have fantasies about rape derive sexual pleasure from violently controlling their partners and may believe that all women secretly want to be raped.

Sexual Harassment: Sexual harassment of a person includes many subtle and overt behaviors. These behaviors include: Sexist comments, unwelcome attention, violations of personal space, unwelcome verbal sexual advances, unwelcome invitations, unwelcome physical advances, unwelcome explicit sexual propositions, sexual coercion/bribery.

Sexual harassment may be an individual event, a cluster of isolated incidents, or it may be repetitive. It is likely to be most destructive when it is repetitive. Threats and violence are often an extension of sexual harassment, in that they are overt expressions of the more subtle behaviors.

Sexual assault: any forced sexual physical contact short of forced sexual intercourse.

Rape: sexual intercourse against the will and without the consent of a person.

EDUCATING *VS.* BLAMING

Because the primary goal of rape education is prevention, the program should be free of blame in any context. Broad statements such as "all men are potential rapists" can be inflammatory, depending on the individual's moral and social development. Many are not prepared to accept this kind of message. Rather, a discussion free of blame but intended to educate will be most productive.

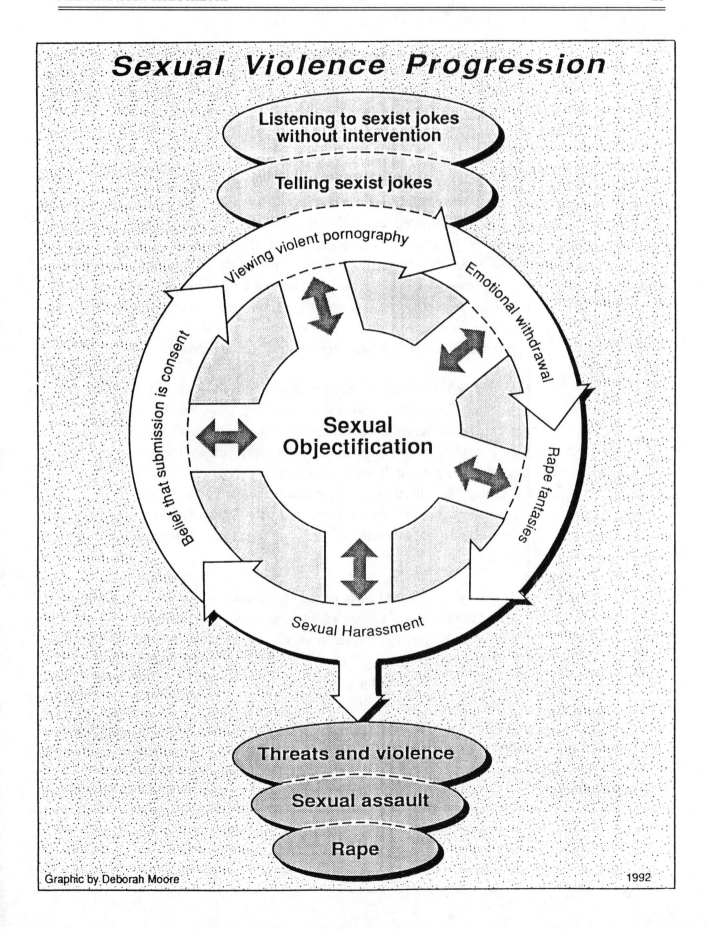

Sexual Violence Progression

Listening to sexist jokes without intervention

Telling sexist jokes

Viewing violent pornography

Emotional withdrawal

Belief that submission is consent

Sexual Objectification

Rape fantasies

Sexual Harassment

Threats and violence

Sexual assault

Rape

Graphic by Deborah Moore

1992

Proactive, Reactive and Punitive Programs

Consider the impetus for the program when devising your plan. A proactive presentation is one where the purpose is strictly prevention. A proactive approach attempts to address the problem before it arises. This is clearly the least threatening type of presentation. Unfortunately, many programs are reactive in that they are arranged in response to an incident such as an assault by a team member. The most challenging are programs which are required as punishment for an offense. With reactive and punitive programs, it is essential that the facilitators do not present themselves as adversaries. Acknowledging that the athletes may resent being required to attend the program can help diffuse the tension which will be present. Furthermore, the players may need an opportunity to express their feelings about the incident. If they do not feel that their side of the story has been heard, their ears will remain closed.

It is also possible that when you are conducting rape prevention programs for athletes, you may be speaking to an accused assailant. This circumstance makes the presentation of the program a tricky finesse. You do not want to be viewed as the enemy, or as the judge and jury, proclaiming the man's guilt. Approach the program carefully by planning a strategy and discussing the problem with the coach. If the program had been planned long before the man was charged, the facilitator should make that clear to the athletes. Simply introduce the program by saying the following:

"We are pleased to have the opportunity to speak to the team this year on the issue of sexual assault prevention. We would like to discuss the issue in general, rather than discussing any particular case. We welcome this opportunity to answer questions and talk about issues that have become increasingly important on college campuses today. As leaders within the college community, we hope you will use this information to improve the campus environment and make it safer for everyone."

If you have conducted programs with the team before, you may add: "We appreciate your thoughtful participation in the past, and are looking forward to another valuable program with you. In order to avoid redundancies, can some of the men who were here for the past programs help to summarize the important points raised in the past two years?''

As a result, the emphasis becomes the continuity of the program and its proactive nature, rather than the guilt or innocence of a member of the team.

Working with all Male Groups

Special care needs to be taken in working with all male groups. Because most educators working in the area of sexual assault prevention are female, and few of the male educators have played college varsity sports, it is difficult to find facilitators with whom the male athletes can relate. It is very important that the trainers are perceived as being there to help them avoid a problem, rather than to point a finger at those "bad boys." Insights about women must come from the facilitators or the other men. This means that the facilitators must be accepted by the group if the group is to hear the message. Therefore, it is preferable to have a male cofacilitator with whom the men can relate.

It is best to have the coach or some of the players co-facilitate the program if they are skilled facilitators, especially if they are respected members of the team. Alternately, if they are not able to facilitate, they may be able to set the stage in a positive way by introducing the program.

■ "Working with African American Male Athletes" by Ron Campbell*

Working with African American male athletes on the issue of sexual violence involves exploring cultural and racial patterns of communication, behavioral expressions of masculinity, masculinity development, and the impact of racism on African American men in America.

Myths and Stereotypes

Once it is understood how some African American men have been socialized, it is possible to make connections between the racist stereotypes of African American males and sexual violence. A closer examination of the stereotypes and how they are used exposes the content of the misinformation that encourages attitudes and behaviors that promote sexual violence.

Many African American male athletes develop coping skills and strategies that allow them to act privileged and then revert to their "real" selves when in a more comfortable setting of their self-selected peers. The result of being bombarded with images and myths about their athletic privilege and sometimes hypersexual activity causes African American males to be what Amos Wilson (1978) describes as being "out of synch." African American male athletes in particular must be made to understand that they will be held to the same or higher standards of behavior as other students.

Several authors (West, 1993; Herenton, 1965; Hooks, 1992; Gary, 1981; Riley, 1987; Bell, 1992) maintain that when we finally begin to really unravel the racism problem and its affects on the character and images of African Americans that we will begin to unravel the sexual violence problem too. Racism, like sexism, has allowed for the formation and perpetuation of myths, lies, and stereotypes about people of color, especially with regard to their sexuality.

---

*Mr. Campbell is Assistant Vice President for Housing and Food Services, University of Minnesota.

Alternative Masculinity

Campus studies of African American men conducted by Worth, et al., (1990); Speas and Thorpe (1979); and Harris (1992) demonstrate that African American men will develop alternative masculinity styles on campus to cope with social pressures. Alternative masculinity styles are the different ways that African American men have found to express their masculinity, when they are presented with a prescribed campus social system that gives them limited and unacceptable choices for their behavioral expressions. African American male athletes might join all white fraternities, engage in exclusive interracial dating, establish negative drinking patterns, dress in exaggerated styles, develop anti-social behavior toward women and men, and exhibit hyper-sexual behavior.

The athletic environment and the special privilege that it carries often contributes to the negative social experiences of African American males. Most African American men on college campuses want to be viewed and defined in context of their identity as a person and not just in terms of their athletic ability. Most African American men are simply seeking places where they see comfortable images of themselves, where they can find acceptance and be respected.

College campuses might begin to understand and change the climate for African American men, Asians, Latinos, Native American Indians, and all men whose cultural identity and masculinity is still challenged by a social system created to empower white men.

African American Masculinity

Masculinity can no longer be defined in culturally singular terms. All of the current literature that focuses on masculinity is based on the white male model and the problems the white male system has caused.

The fact is that men of different racial and ethnic groups have learned about male gender roles and identity differently. Every culture has a definition for masculine behavior that is passed on to males and supported by their entire social system. Learning what each culture teaches about the male role is the work educators have to do in understanding how to support and educate men on our diverse campuses.

In order to support and educate African American male athletes it is important to understand how the role of the African American male has been shaped by current attitudes and behaviors towards women. The historical experience of African American men with African American women has been one of co-dependence and sharing, not the history of pain and abandonment that we are so often showed by the media. Our challenge is to confront the images and problems that are tearing the African American community and society apart, with new images and new ways of learning what it means to be an African American male. We need to have more visible positive role models encouraging relationships that inspire communication and trust. We need to learn and understand the issues of sexual harassment and sexual violence as they have been taught to African American men by the white male social system.

The route for African American males to achieve economic, political and social success in American society is not through the mimicking of sexist behaviors and attitudes. African American males must rediscover their historical and cultural roots to find the real definitions and images of their masculinity. The challenge for African American males in re-defining their masculinity is to ask themselves as men to do "new" things; "new" things that are necessary for the survival of the African American community.

We are asking African American men to develop their communication skills to be able to negotiate solutions with African American women for our relationship problems. We are asking African American males to take time to talk with each other so that they might learn co-dependence is a strength and not a weakness. We are asking African American males to read Afrocentric history books so that they might begin to learn new information that challenges the myths and stereotypes. We are asking African American males to change their language and attitudes towards women and give them respect as valued members of our community. We are asking African American males to try new ideas and learn new ways of being a man. We are asking African American males to reach out and help to mentor someone so that we might continue the chain of advancement of positive ideas and information.

It is important to keep in mind that any solutions offered to African American men for changing behaviors or to be themselves, must give them a reasonable chance to express these behaviors on campus and to take their new behaviors back home. Otherwise the changes will only be temporary and will be discarded when challenged by the more popular, but negative attitudes expressed by their peers. Solutions offered for improving communication and behavior must be attached to cultural values that encourage and support the development of a positive self-esteem and identity. You will be able to identify examples of solutions involving culture once you understand the problems and negative stereotypes of masculinity for the African American population on your campus.

Other examples of solutions involve the utilization of campus resources and academic classes that can provide the African American male athlete with cultural information and a network for peer support. Another solution as a cultural experience is the type of group forum that allows the African American male athlete the opportunity to share their social experience with other men who share their same cultural perspective. This helps not only to bring a community of men closer together, it also validates the experience and helps to eliminate the feelings of isolation that are so commonly reported. The development of real friendships is what many men remember the most from childhood experiences and recreating friendship atmospheres is a forum that can be used for the effective transmittal of new information.

African American Male Resocialization

Socialization is the process by which individuals develop attitudes, expectations, behaviors, values, and skills that coalesce into roles or learned behaviors. Resocialization is the process by which learned information is challenged by new information, providing a basis for values and behaviors to change.

African American men have heard that women are to be used for sex, real men don't ask — they take, it is acceptable to hit women to control them, only the strong survive, and a man must dominate his woman. Our responsibilty as educators is to take this "learned information" and discount the value of it by exposing the misinformation and providing new information regarding masculinity and sexuality.

Exercises and activities may help get men to understand and evaluate the amount of information concerning their masculinity that comes from their sources of influence. This may be accomplished having them discuss how much of the information they use from each source and finally how much of the information they trust. The result is that most men get the most information, and use the most information from sources they trust the least, the media and peers. Most men get and use the least amount of information from sources they trust the most, parents, religion, and schools. If we are going to get new information to African American males we must encourage the sources that they should and do trust the most to become active in our efforts to prevent sexual violence.

The roles for coaches, academic advisors, educators, and parents must be carefully scripted for giving these important messages. These scripts for presenting new information must allow for the continuation of the current relationship between the athlete and the information source. We need to capitalize on the strength of the trust relationship to help make the powerful new information seem less threatening.

At the same time we must understand that the same social situations that allowed for information to be discounted the first time still exists. We as educators must work with parents and others in our communities to re-establish relationships and develop new ways of communicating with young adults. Those of us who are educators and others who have opportunities of influence working with African American male athletes, must examine our own lives and accept the fact that some of our learning has been flawed. Therefore we must experience workshops and programs that will allow us to become supportive role models whose lives are examples of what they are asking others to become.

Suggested Goals for Working with African American Male Athletes

The *first goal* must be to make African American men aware of the existence of the key components of the cultural heritage and customs that effect their masculinity.

The *second goal* is to raise the level of awareness about sexual assault and violence in the African American community on campus. This should also be the opportunity to focus on the legal definition of sexual assault and the special risk for athletes.

The *third goal* is to define strategies that will empower African American males to identify and confront negative attitudes and behaviors towards women and themselves.

The *fourth goal* is to help them make connections between the campus environment and the athletic environment. It is important that the African American male athlete be placed in a situation where he can achieve a realistic balance between athletics and the rest of his life.

I must make mention of several cautions for educators of the majority culture in America to consider if they want to present workshops for African American male athletes. First, you might consider co-presenting or having the workshop presented by an African American if it involves historically sensitive cultural issues with which you are unfamiliar. It is more important to establish credibility for the transmission of critical information, than it is for *you* to present the information. I suggest that majority culture presenters present topics concerning basic sexuality and judicial policies that explore standards of behavior for all students. We, as a society, are still struggling with the dynamics of race and gender and when the interactions of these forces come into our workshops they have an effect on the learning outcome. This effect does not have to be negative, it just means that different information will be shared and there is the possibility for greater social distancing as an outcome.

It is important to remember that workshops for African American male athletes are not substitutes, but that they are in addition to other workshop experiences. Mixed race and/or gender workshops should deal with general topics that concern all groups as it relates to their common experiences as students on a college or university campus.

Conclusion

African American male athletes can and have accepted the responsibilty for working to prevent and understand sexual assault in their own lives. We must make greater efforts to help all men of color eliminate campus and societal based sources of conflict that prevent social and cultural acceptance.

We must use the strength of the dynamics involved in the human relationships forged through athletic competition to support new images of masculinity for all men on campus. All men and women whose positions as sources of influence or information for athletic competition become potential educators. All athletes who share the common experiences of competition or socialization can become capable of sharing and listening to each other. The time they spend together becomes the possible opportunity for new information to be shared.

The perpetuation of the intergenerational and social miseducation of African American male athletes will be interrupted when they become fully empowered to learn, think, and act as well off the playing field as they do on the playing field. As educators we must work hard and become educated ourselves to help African American male athletes take the risk and break through barriers to achieve change.

Akbar, N. 1984. *Chains and Images of Psychological Slavery.* Jersey City, New Jersey: New Mind Productions.

Asante, M.K. 1988. *Afrocentricity.* Trenton, New Jersey: Africa World Press.

Bell, D. 1992. *Faces at the Bottom of the Well: The Permanence of Racism.* New York: Basic Books.

Berkow, D. and R. Page. 1991. "Concepts of the Self: Western and Eastern Perspectives." *Journal of Multicultural Counseling and Development,* 4 (19), 83-93.

Casenave, N.A. 1984. "Race, Socioeconomic Status, and Age: The Social Context of American Masculinity." *Sex Roles,* 11, 639-656.

Coleman, W., Matthews, P. and D. Worth. May 1990. "Sex Role, Group Affiliation, Family Background and Courtship Violence in College Students." *Journal of College Student Development,* 31.

Dyson, Michael, E. 1993. *Reflecting Black: African American Cultural Criticism.* Minneapolis, MN: University of Minnesota Press.

Gary, L.E. 1981. *Black Men.* Beverly Hills, CA: Sage Publications.

Hare, N. and J. Hare. 1984. *The Endangered Black Family: Coping with the Unisexualization and Coming Extinction of the Black Race.* San Francisco, CA: Black Think Tank.

Harris, S. 1992. "Black Male Masculinity and Same Sex Friendships." *Western Journal of Black Studies.* 16 (2), 74-81.

Hernton, C. 1988. *Sex and Racism in America.* New York: Anchor Books Doubleday.

Hooks, B. 1992. *Black Looks Race and Representation.* Boston: South End Press.

Kimmel, M. 1987. *Changing Men: New Direction in Research on Men and Masculinity.* Newbury Park, CA: Sage.

Kochman, T. 1981. *Black and White Styles in Conflict.* Chicago: The University of Chicago Press.

Kunjufu, Lawanza. 1985. *Countering the Conspiracy to Destroy Black Boys.* Chicago: African American Images.

R.C.

■ "Working with Athletes" by Jackson Katz Ed.M.*

When addressing all-male groups of athletes, typically I begin by acknowledging that I'm aware that there might be some guys present who are annoyed and resentful at having to attend a mandatory program on sexual assault. Then I ask their indulgence so we all can make the most of our time together.

I explain, briefly, that I'm not there to blame or attack. I say something like, "Look, guys. I'm not saying that you're a bunch of sexist jerks, and I'm not, so I'm not going to lecture at you. We're all men, we've grown up male in this culture. If we're honest, we have to admit that deep down we all have some pretty sexist attitudes about women, sex and power. That's as true for me as it is for you."

This helps to reduce their defensiveness, which in my experience is a near-universal sentiment among collegiate athletes in discussions about date rape and related topics. I've spoken to racially and socioeconomically diverse groups at Division One schools. I've facilitated workshops with all-white, middle-to-upper class young men at small, prestigious liberal arts schools. I've met with dozens of athletic teams and fraternities.

There are issues of class, race, and local experience that can complicate the discussion. It is important to acknowledge this. Racism is at the root of some of our culture's most powerful rape myths. Refuting these myths (e.g., a disproportionately high percentage of rapes of white women are perpetrated by African-American men) is one of the goals of anti-rape education. In racially diverse groups, it also serves to assure the African-American athletes (male and female) that they won't be scapegoated and that the facilitator has a degree of racial sensitivity.

One of the ways I talk about race is to use analogies between racism and sexism. For example, I'll say, "As a white person, I won't put up with racist jokes from friends, and I couldn't maintain a friendship with someone who was openly racist."

---

*Mr. Katz is Project Coordinator of the Mentors in Violence Prevention (MVP) Project at the Center for the Study of Sport in Society at Northeastern University.

"Most of us," I continue, "can see how racist jokes reflect and perpetuate the kinds of attitudes that contribute to discrimination and violence against real people. It's not simply harmless fun." Most of the student-athletes I've spoken with — primarily white and African-American — readily accept this line of reasoning.

"So what's the difference," I ask, "when guys tell sexist jokes or make degrading comments about women?" I mention that in the United States battering is the leading cause of injury to women. If attitudes influence actions when it comes to racism, why not with sexism as well?

While I address the class and race subject, I make a point of emphasizing what unites us: the fact that we're males in a society with an outrageously high level of male violence against women.

This allows me to highlight the central theme of my presentation, which is that in our society we have had a severe shortage of leadership from men on the subject of sexism and all forms of men's violence against women. I explain that I'm not there to criticize student athletes for contributing disproportionately to the problem. Rather, I'm there to appeal to their instincts for leadership on a very difficult issue.

At that point in the program, in some groups, I introduce an exercise. I distribute a blank piece of paper to each guy, and ask them to write, on one side, what they would like to say to women about the subject of sex, men, relationships, rape, or other forms of abuse and violence. I tell them to picture a roomful of attentive women. What would they say to these women? Here's your chance to explain how you feel . . . and it's anonymous.

On side two I ask them to tell me what qualities they admire and respect in themselves or in other men. What adjectives would they like others to use describing them, either now or in the future? I explain that their responses will be used to facilitate later discussion.

Then I talk about the problem I see in describing issues like rape, sexual assault, harassment, and battering as "women's issues." It gives guys an excuse not to pay attention, allows us to think that these are things that only women have to be concerned with. But that's a fallacy.

To demonstrate this, I say, "By a show of hands, how many of you guys have either sisters, girlfriends, wives, mothers, or grandmothers?" This precipitates laughter and some snickers, but all the guys raise their hands. I ask them if they see my point: that every issue which affects the women and girls that they care about affects them by definition. This is not a men-against-women thing. We're all in this together. We use the same bathrooms, sleep in the same beds. Our lives are inextricably interwoven with each other.

Every woman who is raped or assaulted by a man is someone's sister, daughter, or friend. I tell them to keep this in mind as we discuss the issue. How would you feel if your girlfriend awoke in the night screaming and punching the pillow after a nightmarish flashback to her assault?

Part of my approach in addressing any population of students, athletes or not, is to emphasize that we're in the midst of a crisis of man's violence against women in this society. I think it is necessary to emphasize this because many of us have been desensitized to the extent of the violence through constant exposure in the entertainment media as well as the news.

In mixed gender groups I've used an exercise that has proven very useful in demonstrating the pervasiveness of the violence. I draw a line down the middle of a blackboard and put a female symbol on one side and a male symbol on the other. Then I ask for the men only to tell me what steps they take, on a daily basis, to prevent themselves from being sexually assaulted.

Usually there is some giggling and commotion. Sometimes a guy raises his hand and makes a sarcastic comment. Eventually someone says "nothing." Then I ask the same question of the women. Invariably their list goes on for several minutes, typically filling up both sides of the blackboard. Women report carrying mace or rape whistles, checking the back seat of their car before getting in, listing their first initial in the phone book, not stopping at rest areas on highways, not making eye contact with strange men, etc.

One reason this exercise is effective is that a lot of guys have never thought about how dramatically women's lives are affected by the risk and threat of men's violence.   The cluttered blackboard is a stark visual reminder that I and others in the room can refer to repeatedly in the course of the discussion. In racially diverse groups, it also helps to demonstrate to white male students another way that their gender privilege complements their skin color privilege.   (In presentations I've done, African-American men have been the only men who've raised their hands when I've asked how many men do things like look in the back seat of the car, called friends to say they've arrived someplace safely, etc.)

The content of the middle portion of my workshop and presentations to athletes varies. Sometimes I focus on rape and sexual assault issues. Sometimes the meeting has been called because of an incident of sexual harassment, and we need to pursue that specific issue more thoroughly. Battering has increasingly been a topic of conversation.

But usually I touch briefly on all of them because they're all linked. And I always talk about the media because the media is crucial in the construction of violent masculinity and in perpetrating the myth that the rape and murder of young, attractive women is sexually stimulating or "erotically thrilling."

Toward the latter part of the program I read some of the responses from their earlier exercise. For example, many of the guys want women to know that "not all men are rapists or sexist pigs." I use this to make the point that if you feel that way, you have to speak out, because if men who don't abuse women are silent, other men take our silence as a form of consent.

And it's not enough to interrupt physical violence. We also have to confront and radicate sexist attitudes, in ourselves and our peers. These attitudes lead to violence because they degrade and dehumanize women.

Reading these responses is a good device to spark discussion. It's also a good way to keep people's attention, because although it's anonymous, many students want to hear their contributions read aloud.

I use the last part of the exercise as a way to wrap up the discussion. Most guys list qualities like strength, courage, and leadership as things they aspire to. I affirm this and then apply it to this subject. Alluding back to the beginning of the program, I emphasize that what we've been lacking in this society is men who have the courage to stand up and speak out against sexism.

I remind the guys that they all have girls and women about whom they care deeply. And I acknowledge that there is a lot of pressure on young guys to conform to group norms of masculinity. Guys who confront abusive peers are taking a risk. Their masculinity might be questioned or their sexuality. Homophobia causes a lot of guys to remain silent. But leadership is about taking risks.

I close with an analogy from my sports experience to which most of the men can relate. My coaches used to say that if we didn't give 110 percent, we're the only ones who have to look ourselves in the mirror the next morning. The analogy applies to this subject as well. Women in our generation have to live with so much violence. From the men close to them — their boyfriends, friends and classmates — to the psychopaths lurking in the shadows. I point to the blackboard for emphasis.

I stress that as men, we're in a position to do something about it. Especially as athletes. I remind them that their peers look up to them. They're role models whether they've consciously chosen to be or not. They have a choice to make: to stand up and speak out against race and all forms of sexism, or to remain silent.

I tell them that they'll probably never see me again and who knows how they feel about me and what I had to say. But it really doesn't matter. What matters is when they look in the mirror. Will they be able to look at themselves in the eye and say that they're doing all they can to make the world a safer place for the girls and women they love? Will they be able to hold their head high?

J.K.

■ "Rape Prevention Programs for Athletes: Special Characteristics of NCAA Division I Athletic Departments" by Tom Jackson, Ph.D.*

This segment addresses what are believed to be the special considerations and needs a facilitator must consider in order to effectively conduct a rape prevention program in a NCAA Division I athletic department. The recommendations presented here are the result of experience with numerous rape prevention presentations to Div. I athletic departments, consultation with and presentations to the NCAA, and informal discussions with athletic directors, coaches, and athletes over the last five years. Prior to addressing the recommended characteristics of and considerations for facilitators, the typical demographics of the athletic departments in question will be presented. NCAA Div. I athletic departments are almost always housed in large colleges and universities. The average undergraduate enrollment in these institutions is typically between fifteen and thirty thousand, and the average athletic department budget is typically between five and twenty million dollars a year. People who have worked around these Div. I departments know that what we are talking about here is "big-time college athletics." There is no easy way to capture in words the fanatacism of those who are involved with or root for these teams and departments in this division. Big-time college athletics has clearly evolved into a phenomenon much larger than the academic institution which houses it; spawning intense, sometimes rabid intra- and interstate, regional, and oftentimes national rivalries. This situation results in the conferring of a "special status" on such student athletes. These young men become "personalities" within their colleges, communities, states, and even nationally. This special status is instilled by the coaches and fans and not surprisingly is subscribed to by the athletes themselves (Jackson, 1992).

Before discussing individual athlete demographics, an important distinction must be made within these athletic departments among the various individual sports and teams. Extensive differences have been found between the revenue-generating team sports (football and basketball) and all other team and individual sports. For example, while self-reported male athlete sexual assault perpetration rates for an entire Div. I athletic department may not differ significantly when compared to

*Dr. Jackson is Professor of Psychology, University of Arkansas.

those of non-athlete male students, football and basketball athletes report significantly more assaultive behaviors than athletes in other sports (Jackson, 1991). The potential reasons for these differences may lie in the type of competitive drive, levels of aggression, win-at-all-cost philosophy, and "in-group/out-group" mentality of these two types of teams. Further, enormous pressure is brought to bear on athletes and coaches, especially those involved in football and basketball, to succeed. This pressure comes from students, the college or university, boosters, fans, and the entire state in cases. This pressure, and the resulting hostility and negative press that occurs when absolute success is not attained, serves to isolate further the two types of teams. It is my contention that this isolation and "us *versus* them" mentality lessens the possibility of outsiders having an educational impact on NCAA Div. I football and basketball teams. This is why it is critically important to have the support of the athletic director and coaches prior to initiating rape prevention programs for athletes.

The student/athlete makeup of the aforementioned teams is typically as follows. First, the representation of ethnic groups within Div. I football and basketball teams is different from other sports, such that there is typically a significant African American majority of athletes on these teams. Second, the socioeconomic background is decidedly lower for these athletes than for student/athletes involved in other sports or NCAA divisions. Third, almost all of the football and basketball athletes in Div. I are on scholarship. Fourth, basketball and football athletes more often have a history of single-parent upbringing than athletes from other teams or divisions. Fifth, it appears that the mean high school GPAs and college entrance examination scores for Division I football and basketball scholarship athletes are somewhat lower than those of other teams or divisions. Sixth, a final characteristic of these athletes that serves to separate them from others is their physical prowess. Football and basketball Div. I scholarship athletes are typically taller, stronger, more powerful, and generally more easily recognizable than their non-athlete peers. This "differentness" is exacerbated by the significantly special status accorded these athletes that was mentioned earlier.

With regard to coaches' attitudes towards sexual assault, a range of responses may be expected within and between the staff at these athletic departments. This range is anchored on one end by sensitive, education and prevention oriented coaches who are strongly and genuinely supportive of rape education programs. The other anchor point for coaches' attitudes is best typified by the basketball coach who, when told his players had participated in a group rape, replied, boys will be boys.

This range of staff attitudes argues for facilitators conducting a pre-training assessment of coaches and athletic department staff attitudes and levels of support involving rape education.

Essentially, I believe that the rape prevention programs presented in this manual are most useful for athletes in all sports from colleges other than Div. I, as well as for those Div. I athletes from non-revenue generating team sports. It is my strong contention that Division I basketball and football teams should be approached differently. The remainder of this section will delineate the recommended differences, focusing almost exclusively on Div. I football and basketball teams.

Characteristics of an appropriate rape prevention facilitator: Given the subject matter and the above specialized audience characteristics, a number of concrete facilitator characteristics are strongly recommended. The facilitator must necessarily feel comfortable with open discussions of sex and other sensitive topics. They must also be comfortable speaking in front of large (pun intended), and oftentimes hostile, groups. Facilitators who have previously experienced considerable success in presenting their programs to receptive (or at least "lukewarm") audiences may be taken aback by the hostile reception provided by these athletes. A common reaction of facilitators is to feel degraded and, in a way, victimized by the overpowering force that is represented by a Division I football team. Keeping calm and non-defensive as a speaker is critical, as is the ability to defuse angry and sometimes primitive interchanges expressing conflicting values and ideas. An example of this type of interchange involves a facilitator suggesting that athletes communicate their desires for sexual interaction, to which a football player replied, "Shit man, nobody asks for pussy anymore." It is important to be able to use the vocabulary and empathize with the experience of the audience, while calmly pointing out the possible horrific contingencies of the "boys will be boys" mentality. Thirdly, in this specific case, the facilitator will be much more successful if they are knowledgeable regarding college athletics, either through previous involvement in college athletics, an awareness of the specific athletic department's history and current standings, or through being in good physical condition themselves. Finally, it is strongly recommended that at least one of the facilitators be male. Female facilitators can be easily dismissed as "man-haters," "rabid feminists," or simply as "women" by male athletes. The message can be easily lost due to the medium. If a male, especially one seen by the athletes as a "powerful" male is a co-facilitator, the message is much less likely ignored. If at all possible, it is recommended that a former athlete; a coach, or an athletic department official be used as an additional co-facilitator to corroborate statements made during the formal program (Carroll & Jackson, in press).

Special considerations for facilitators with this sample: There are a number of recommendations regarding the process of providing rape education programming to NCAA Division I athletic departments (Jackson, 1992). First, prior to presenting any program within an athletic department, it is critically important to have the support of the athletic director and coaches. There is simply no other issue that creates greater potential for failure with this audience than the facilitator being seen as an "outsider." My presentations to Division I athletic departments have all been at the invitation of the athletic director.

Second, it is strongly recommended that the athletic director make attendance at the program mandatory. If possible, the program can be credited as study hall or continuing education. As is always the case, if attendance is voluntary, the individuals who need it the most do not attend.

Third, it is recommended that the rape education program be presented to these male athletes in isolation. Female athletes or other non-athlete groups tend to dilute the message and diminish the potential for significant interaction by their presence. If possible it is recommended that the football team be provided with a program by itself. In this way the "specialness" of the team can be preserved and, in fact, used to make points more salient.

Fourth, I have found it critical for facilitators to use recent examples of athletes and athletic departments that have been implicated in or accused of assault, and the resulting consequences. The increased salience of "name" athletes that have been jailed and programs whose reputations have been tarnished is palpable during the presentation. Often, pointing out that "bad news sells," the "higher you are ranked in the NCAA, the harder you fall in the media," and that even the rumor of sexual assault can cost an athlete positions in the draft or his potential future career is relevant (Carroll & Jackson, in press).

Finally, with regard to content, it is recommended that excessive role playing and other structured activities that could be perceived as "phoney" or "uncool" be avoided at all costs. From my experience in working with these athletes, you have succeeded in your efforts if the following goals are accomplished: 1) basic information regarding sexual assault is presented, including the costs involved; and 2) through role playing, you have impressed upon these athletes the necessity for sexually assertive communication and have expanded their repertoire of "lines" to ask for sex in a non-coercive or assaultive manner (Jackson, 1992).

Carroll, K. & T. Jackson (in press). "Rape education and prevention training: Special presentations." In T. Jackson (Ed.) *A mental health practitioner's guide to dealing with acquaintance rape.* Sarasota, FL: Professional Resource Press, Inc.

Jackson, T. 1991. "A university athletic department's rape and assault experiences." *Journal of College Student Development,* 32, 77-78.

Jackson, T. 1992, October. *Rape Education and Prevention Programs for Athletic Departments.* International Conference on Sexual Assault on Campus, Orlando, FL.

T.J.

Summary

As can be seen from the above, it is strongly recommended that special considerations be made when presenting rape education programs to NCAA Division I athletic departments. These considerations include: separating male and female athletes; separating football and basketball athletes from all others; having the strong support of the athletic director; making attendance at the program mandatory for the athletes; pre-training sessions with coaches and athletic department personnel; and keeping the amount of role-playing and structured activities to a minimum. For facilitators, recommendations include: having a male co-facilitator; being comfortable with physically imposing, aggressive, and primitive audiences; having a working knowledge of athletics; using an athlete, coach, or the athletic director as an informal co-facilitator; and being able to stay calm, non-defensive, and facilitative in the presence of one of the last true bastions of pure male aggression and machismo left in our society.

There is powerful anecdotal evidence regarding the effectiveness of the above program. In one example, several athletes missed a presentation due to scheduling difficulties. These were the only athletes implicated in sexual offenses in this large athletic department over the five years that this rape education program was in place. Athletes in this department who attended the presentation unanimously agreed that the implicated athletes would not have engaged in the alleged behavior had they also attended the program (Jackson, 1992).

The potential for failure is great when the above recommendations are not followed. Several facilitators have reported feeling degraded, dehumanized, and victimized as a result of "being thrown to the wolves." However, when the athletic department is supportive of the rape education and prevention program, and when a modicum of common sense and care is taken when working with this very special population, the result can be one of the most rewarding experiences a facilitator can have.

PLANNING A PROGRAM: LOGISTICS

The following discussion outlines a framework for planning sexual assault education programs specifically for the male college athlete. This framework is successful with both contact and non-contact sports teams.

With few adaptations, similar methods may be effective with co-ed audiences. It is always useful for men to hear what women think about this issue, and vice-versa. Because co-ed programs are potentially more volatile, facilitator's must be well prepared to prevent discussions from turning into angry, defensive and unconstructive debates.

If the flexibility exists, there is value in conducting two programs; one for the men alone, and then one with women present. This provides a safe environment for discussion initially, but then allows for challenges to further the men's feelings about this emotional topic.

CONDUCT A NEEDS ASSESSMENT

At the outset, it is important to learn about the team that will be participating in the program. Talking to coaches, team captains or other players to identify special needs or characteristics of the team will help provide information to which a program can be tailored. Learning about the sport and the kinds of dynamics it requires, such as the degree of aggression and the extent of teamwork involved, can provide information about the training the team has experienced.

It is most important to identify professional men who can facilitate the programs and whose experiences will contribute to these kinds of programs. At Cornell, a male educator who was a college football player and a member of a fraternity co-facilitated the programs. His familiarity with the sports language and the anecdotes from his college years were invaluable contributions to the program. Having been a member of a high status team during his college years helped boost his credibility (and by association the credibility of his co-facilitators) with the players.

CHAPTER 5

If available, additional details about the team's extracurricular activities should be compiled prior to any presentations: What is the level of alcohol use by the team? Do most of the players belong to a particular fraternity? Has the fraternity ever been cited for sexual harassment or associated issues? Is there a particular group, male and/or female, with whom the team socializes? What social restrictions are implemented when the team is "in-season?" Use this information to tailor the program.

IDENTIFY FACILITATORS

Having a skilled facilitator with previous collegiate or pro sport experience is not always possible. However, athletes with a commitment to the issue of sexual assault prevention can learn to co-lead effective presentations even if they are not professional educators. For example, we once recruited a facilitator with semi-pro football experience and asked him to support our ideas during the program, rather than actually deliver the message. Although he did not have particular expertise in sexual assault education, he did have a commitment to the issue and was willing to learn and work with two female co-facilitators who are well versed in sexual assault prevention, but not so well versed in the needs of male athletes. The female co-facilitators presented the material on sexual assault, and he presented information on the social pressures athletes may experience such as peer pressure to participate in sexual harassment or gang rape. His presence and input lent credibility to the overall program.

You may also want to consider recruiting future facilitators from teams you address. Be on the alert for insightful and enlightened participants in your programs who are natural leaders, and who seem to garner the respect of their teammates. These men may require some one-on-one training to introduce them to facilitation concepts but the pay-off is likely to be tremendous. These new recruits are not likely to be available until their sport is out-of-season, but once they are free they will be able to provide new information to you which will likely make future programs even more successful than past programs.

■   **"The University of Maine**
     Athletes for Sexual Responsibility"
     by Sandy Caron*

Here at the University of Maine sexual assault/rape education of athletes is provided by the peer education program I direct: Athletes for Sexual Responsibility. This program was established in 1990 to supplement the already existing Peer Educator Program which has been in existence since the mid-1970's. Unlike the Peer Educator Program, which recruits students from the general student body, Athletes for Sexual Responsibility members are all student-athletes. We have approximately 25 male and female student-athletes representing all intercollegiate sports at the University of Maine. As the Director of the program, I work closely with the Athletic Department in terms of support and recruitment of new members. Margaret Zillioux, Associate Athletic Director for Academic Support, serves as the athletic liaison to the program.

Athletics at University of Maine: The University of Maine has 19 intercollegiate varsity sports (ice hockey and baseball are nationally recognized). There are 450 - 500 student-athletes (2% of which are minority); 228 students are on athletic scholarships. It should be noted that the GPA and graduation rate for student-athletes has been consistently comparable or higher than that of the general student body. They are seen as "student-athletes" *versus* just "athletes." I am not aware of any special treatment or privileges they may receive; if anything, it seems they are often discriminated against or held to a higher standard than other students. In terms of sexual assault, no team has a reputation for 'being rapists." In fact, of all the rapes reported (and those rapes I am aware of which were never reported) in the past 5 years I have been at this university, none have involved athletes. In terms of the coaches attitudes toward sexual assault, most are quite knowledgeable. They support education in this area and have always been open to presentations on this topic for themselves and their players. We have full support for our program from the Athletic Director to the coaches and other staff.

Why Peer Education?: We chose the peer education "route" to educate students about rape for several reasons. As students are often the most knowledgeable people on campus about other students, it seemed logical to develop an education program using students as the primary

---

*Dr. Caron is a professor of Human Development at the University of Maine.

deliverers of the prevention message. Student-athletes were chosen because they play a visible role on campus. They are used to being in the spotlight, both on and off the court. We use athletes because they can be important role models on campus. They often set the standard for other students. While not all people look up to athletes, it is recognized that a large number of college students do and this program attempts to capitalize on this interest. Athletes for Sexual Responsibility offers student-athletes a unique opportunity to contribute to community service; allowing them to be a positive role model for other athletes, as well as for other students. In addition, rape is a "touchy" issue; I have noticed that, during a presentation, males will often become defensive and feel like they are being accused of rape. By using male athletes to educate others it is harder for audience members to become defensive — especially when one of your own peers is presenting the information.

Why Rape: When I first established the program 3-1/2 years ago, we decided to begin with one topic which we felt was of most interest and in need of the greatest education: Rape Awareness. After spending almost an entire semester brainstorming the issues surrounding, rape, we narrowed our focus to three themes: 1) Date rape, 2) Gang rape, and 3) How to talk with a friend who has been raped. We designed an interactive workshop around these three themes.

The Workshop: The workshop begins with an overview on rape, followed by a series of three brief vignettes performed by the student-athletes. The first vignette, *The Date,* portrays a male and female whose assumptions and poor communication at the end of a date lead to acquaintance rape. The second and third skits portray attitudes and assumptions held by some students following a gang rape. In the second skit, *The Morning After,* a male involved in a gang rape at a party the night before is bragging to his friend. The friend goes along with his buddy's actions, making the erroneous assumption that the woman must have wanted or invited the assault. The final skit, *Talking With Friends,* involves two friends (a male and female) talking with the victim of the gang rape, but they are not supportive. They question her motives and her dress and suggest that somehow she encouraged the attack.

At a critical point in each of the vignettes, the facilitator steps in, talks with the audience about each predicament and generates alternative ways they can be resolved. The students in the audience give their suggestions, which the players use to rework the skits to end in a positive way. For example, in the last skit, *Talking With Friends,* many students in the audience notice that the victim's friends are not very supportive; the two essentially blame her for the rape, tell her to pretend it never happened, and are generally unsympathetic. The audience provides suggestions for how to rework the skit to show how more supportive friends might respond. In their discussion with the audience, the facilitators emphasize the powerful positive or negative effects that peer attitudes can have in shaping or altering attitudes and assumptions.

Presentations are made to all incoming athletes in the fall. In addition, we have presented our workshop in the residence halls, fraternities and sororities, and to other Maine colleges and high schools. Our hope is that, in addition to educating others about rape, we can break down some of the stereotypes surrounding student-athletes and show that they can be good role models for appropriate behavior. Note: The Rape Awareness workshop is available on video.

It should be noted that last year we expanded our program to include a second workshop focusing on HIV/AIDS called "Smart Sex." (also available on video). Next year we plan to design a third workshop on "Drinking and Dating."

S.C.

GARNERING SUPPORT AND
"SELLING" THE PROGRAM

Coaches (and often athletic directors, department heads, deans or other administrators) play a crucial role in establishing credibility and support for this kind of programming. For those coaches who may resist the idea of rape prevention programming, it may be necessary to appeal to a concern for the team's well-being, safety and role model function in the college community. If there is significant resistance to the program, efforts may be wasted on the resistant coaches, and may even jeopardize future efforts. Also, a coach can easily reverse a program's positive impact if he holds beliefs or attitudes that conflict with what the athletes hear during a program. It would be better initially to find a supportive coach who will welcome these programs, and to create a supportive environment before starting this kind of work.

Should the opportunity arise, approaching a coach informally may have the most successful outcome. Educators should try to schedule a short meeting or approach him after a department meeting. The athletic department may be willing to schedule an inservice-training for coaches at which time educators can address the importance of this kind of program for athletes. If a coach's resistance is low, a supportive athletic director or trainer may be able to convince a coach of the program's merit.

Once one successful program has been conducted for one team, the requests may snowball. At Cornell, the enthusiasm for the football team's program caught the attention of the rowing coach who decided to request a program for his team. A rape education segment was then included in the health education course for varsity athletes which reached men and women from all of the varsity teams.

Coaches can be encouraged to promote rape prevention among their athletes in a variety of ways. Arranging a program by visiting educators or team members is an important step, as is adequately punishing offenders who come to his attention. Moreover, coaches can act as role models by not tolerating language and behaviors that objectify or demean women or are homophobic in nature.

Programs for athletes will be most successful if the coaches believe that the program is important and that they have the support of at least some of the older, respected athletes on the team. Based on the premise that team members should watch out for each other and "do the right thing," rape education should promote the fundamentals familiar to most team players, including the kinds of values that should be instilled in all young men; honesty, respect for others, sincerity and equality. Cornell's Coach Jim Hofher, sends a letter to each member of his incoming football team explaining the kinds of behaviors he expects, that they should "do the right thing" or they will not be part of the team. Coach Hofher refers to not abusing alcohol, drugs, steroids, or people. He also lets the team know that if they encounter one of their fellow athletes behaving inappropriately, they should intervene to stop the inappropriate action. Sexual assault education promotes these principles and is an opportunity to reinforce the kinds of values Coach Hofher expects from his players.

An illustration of an outline of the selling points for providing sexual assault education to team members and that can be given directly to coaches or athletic directors can be found in *Appendix P*.

DESIGNING A FOUR-YEAR CYCLE

Ideally, rape prevention efforts should include a series of programs that address interrelated issues including but not limited to relationship expectations, sexual entitlement, gender roles, power dynamics, communication, and alcohol use. It is best to develop a sequential series of programs based on a 4 year cycle (to coincide with a 4 year degree program) that introduce fundamental concepts (such as assumptions about sexual messages, listening to a woman who says "no," and the law) and then add additional issues that supplement the basics during each subsequent program. It is important to reinforce the basic messages in a new, creative way each year to reach the newer team members who may not have been present during prior programs, while keeping the men who were present at previous programs engaged.

The following brief outline presents ideas for a four-year plan, based on one education meeting per year.

Year One

1)   Coach introduces program

2) Show "She's Only 16" (Santa Monica Rape Treatment, public
    service announcement; see *Appendix B*)

    Discussion: Rape myths.

    What does "no" mean?

    What could have given the man the feeling that it was ok to
    have sex with the player's sister?

    Are there any circumstances under which it is okay to force a
    woman to have sex?

    Why do you think resistance is ignored in these circumstances?

3) Facilitators read "Internal Dialogue" *(Appendix G)*

    Discussion including the alcohol connection

4) Alternate ways of thinking and acting

5) What the law says

6) What to do if it happens to someone you know

Year Two

1) Coach's introduction: athletes are role models

2) Incomplete sentences *(Appendix C):* reviews basic concepts

3) Interactive theater scene:

    Actors present a scenario that ends in rape

    Discussion: Actors stay in role and answer questions from
    audience (covers assorted issues such as sexual entitlement,
    alcohol use, and gender role expectations)

4) Return to incomplete sentence responses

Discussion

5) Review the law

6) What can you do to prevent rape

7) What you can do if it happens to someone you know

Year Three

1) Review: What have you learned from previous year's sessions?

2) Graffiti wall *(Appendix F)*

3) Discussion: What does being a (football, hockey, lacrosse) player mean to you?

   How does it affect your plans for the future?

   What could a sexual assault charge do to those plans?

4) Review & discuss the graffiti wall responses

   Talk about the language that supports rape prone culture ("score," "bang her")

5) Review the law

Year Four

1) Review: What have you learned from previous year's sessions?

2) Team relationship: what makes a team? How does peer pressure affect what team members may do?

3) The association of groups of athletes and gang rape: discussion

4) Gang Rape film clips *(Casualties of War, The Accused)* Discussion

5)   Empathy building:

Victim Testimony (video, written & read)

Discussion

6)   Review how to respond if someone you know is assaulted

To some degree, the first year's program is the most important. Not only will it set the tone for future presentations, but it should intrigue and educate the athletes enough for them to be willing to continue participating in future years. As the players get older, we want them to believe in the importance of this education and act as role models for the younger players. A poorly received program the first year could eliminate the opportunity to meet with the team in subsequent years. Or even if you have the opportunity to return, there will be added resistance that will pose obstacles to a useful discussion. There is nothing worse for a facilitator than facing a moaning, groaning group of uncooperative students! *Appendix O* is a fully developed agenda for a first year basic rape prevention program.

SCHEDULING AND ENVIRONMENT

Schedule the program for a time that maximizes the potential for absorbing information. Try to schedule the program during the team's "off season" or pre-season. Avoid offering the programs during final exam weeks or midterm periods. If the program is to be held during the late afternoon, a comfortable environment and snacks will increase the likelihood of interesting discussion and interaction.

PUBLICIZING: RAPE *VS.* SEX

Mandatory programs for athletes demonstrate a commitment to preventing sexual assault on campus. However, if mandatory programming is not an option, program titles should be so intriguing as to interest the majority of the target group. If the program is to be advertised and introduced as one about sexual assault, the coach may help set the stage by discussing famous athletes who have been arrested and convicted for acquaintance rape. The coaches' support is very important in assuring that the athletes understand the importance of programming on this issue.

Titles for programs which have worked well include:

- Is Alcohol An Aphrodisiac?

- Sex: How To Get Want You Want But Not More Than You Bargained For

- Sex, Lies, and Stereotypes

Planning Follow-up

The program should be evaluated and the results shared with the coach. A call to thank him and offer your services for the next year would be appropriate, along with a summary of evaluation results. Asking the coach for feedback from the athletes as well as his ideas for future programs is a good idea.

To help the coach reinforce the messages conveyed during the program, it may help to provide him with a card bearing a few simple messages. You might suggest that he read them aloud when players are heading our to their post-game parties or tack them on the locker room bulletin board. The following summarize some of the main points for the athletes to remember:

- Your behavior reflects on the whole team.

- Don't force anyone to drink or have sex.

- Stop when you hear "no."

In some cases, it may be possible to contact the team captains or other students willing to talk to you after a program. Facilitators could pass around a sign up sheet or leave one for students when they exit. Athletes could leave their name and phone number if they are willing to be contacted. In addition to being the most accurate measure of the effectiveness of the program, they may be interested in helping to plan another program or the one for the next year. Their support may help ease any difficulties with newer team members the following season.

CONDUCTING A PROGRAM: TECHNIQUES

Before embarking on any rape education program, considerable thought should be given to the goals of the presentation. The goals should be clearly identified in order to prevent false expectations and poor evaluations. While facilitators may hope that a program will keep men from perpetrating sexual violence, in reality, a one or two hour educational program will never provide that assurance. However, realistic goals will provide a framework that will make a program as effective as it can be.

DEFINING GOALS: WHAT IS REALISTIC AND WHAT IS ESSENTIAL?

By realistically defining goals, facilitators clarify what is essential to accomplish during the time allotted and focus the direction of the discussions. Sexual assault is a "loaded" topic; it is easy to be distracted by detailed questions, waylaid by defensive comments and disheartened by victim-blaming statements. Clear goals will help prevent the discussion from veering off track for too long.

During a first-time program, one realistic goal may be simply to inform the participants about rape laws. Or one goal may be to help athletes think critically about the way cultural forces influence behaviors. Maybe there was a well known incident on campus that would make a good case study for discussion. We all know our students best, and educators should never present generic programs, but rather tailor goals and objectives to the athletes involved.

The following goals are an example of those designed for an introductory program on acquaintance rape:

- Understand acquaintance rape, its frequency in the community, and how it is related to force, threat of force, or coercion.

- Understand the role aggression training plays in increasing the likelihood of a sexual assault.

- Explore feelings about sexual assault.

CHAPTER 6

- Explore cultural forces that contribute to the frequency and social "acceptability" of acquaintance rape and sexual assault.

- Understand the contribution of inconsistent verbal and non-verbal communication patterns to acquaintance rape situations.

- Identify prevention strategies and become empowered to work toward the elimination of acquaintance rape and sexual assault in your community.

- Know the laws regarding sexual assault, and the consequences of violating those laws.

Whatever the goals may be, follow them with clearly stated objectives that are behaviorally defined. For example, one objective may be that the men will be able to define rape myths, or be able to name three ways to help prevent rape.

Since the most empowering part of any program is the modeling of appropriate behaviors, it is imperative that this section be presented before any audience members leave. One way to provide them with prevention strategies is to challenge them to think of which behaviors addressed in the program could be incorporated into their already successful repertoire of interactions.

DECISIONS TO MAKE BEFOREHAND

Motive for Program

Once goals have been established, consider the tone you would like the presentation to have. Many considerations shape the program climate. Is the program punitive or mandatory? Do you have the support of the coach? Were you invited or required to present the program to the team?

Don't Lecture

Regardless of the reason for the program, one guideline should be adhered to if possible: Facilitate discussion rather than lecture at students.

However, "mini" lectures can work within the context of a facilitated discussion. If you plan on "reading the riot act" to a team without discussion, activities, or interaction among team members, you are sure to doom the program. Students spend many hours a day in lecture classes and don't want to meet with their team in a classroom climate. Students learn best from one another, so activities that foster discussion will be the most dynamic and educational.

Vary Activities

Variety throughout the cycle is important not only to keep interest, but to ensure that the messages are absorbed. People learn according to different methods. For example, some absorb information better through visual means; large sheets of newsprint paper with important points printed on it ahead of time, or printed handouts are most effective here. Others absorb information easily through mini-lecture and discussion. Varied format will accommodate the differences to be sure everyone is absorbing something important.

The size of a team may affect the quality of planned discussions. For example, educators must decide whether they are comfortable leading and, more importantly, controlling a discussion with a group of 100. Some activities may lend themselves to small group discussion that can then be processed in the larger group afterward. Some men may be more honest and outspoken in small groups.

Have a Contingency Plan

It would also be wise to have a "Plan A" and a "Plan B." Consider all of the things that could go wrong with a program and it is likely that something will come true. Do not rely on any one activity or format, or your plans will most certainly go awry. At one program for the Cornell varsity football team, we designed a discussion around a public service video. When we arrived, we checked the video in the VCR (thinking of Murphy's Law). There was picture but no sound. The VCR was used by the Athletics Department for training films, and the sound cable had been removed. We hadn't planned an alternate discussion to kick off the program, so the male facilitator had to narrate while the video ran. Because we did not have a contingency plan ready, the video was not as effective as we'd hoped.

The Coach Option

Should the coach be present during the program? To best accomplish the program goals, the answer is probably no. However, this decision is situation specific. There may be a circumstance in which the athletes and coach have an extremely open relationship and the coach's presence would not diminish honest discussion. This is probably the exception rather than the rule. However, you are there doing a program at the coach's request, or at the very least with the coach's acknowledgment. Therefore, if he wants to be present, plan the program accordingly. Facilitators can still provide important information without expecting much free, honest discussion from the players because of the coaches presence.

■ **"The Role of Coaches in Rape Prevention
Programs for Athletes"
by Alan Berkowitz, Ph.D.***

Recent empirical research on the effectiveness of rape prevention programs for men have called into question their effectiveness. These studies suggest that men's attitudes may not change as a result of educational interventions and that some program formats may actually reinforce attitudes and beliefs associated with rape proclivity. Athletes and other members of close-knit, cohesive groups of men may be particularly resistant to such interventions because of the strength of group norms, interactions, and emotional bonding.

One variable associated with program effectiveness is the support and advocacy of individuals who are respected and credible to the participants. Among athletes, the role of the coach is crucial. Coaches must ally themselves with the change process initiated by such workshops if the workshops are to be effective. The enormous amount of influence that coaches have on their athletes is well known. Coaches serve as positive role models and often take a personal interest in the lives and well-being of their athletes, providing encouragement and motivation for academic and other extra-curricular activities and often serving as a personal counselor and confidant. Yet male coaches are themselves the product of traditional male socialization processes which inculcate rape supportive attitudes, behaviors, and perceptions, and they can easily undermine rape prevention programs by making derogatory comments, criticizing campus judicial procedures, promoting rape myths, or by making sexist and objectifying remarks about women. In both their actions and speech, coaches serve as powerful agents of socialization into traditional gender roles and attitudes, serving as positive role models in many respects, but often unwittingly reinforcing the beliefs systems which make men more likely to commit rape and sexual assault as well. The role of these socio-cultural factors in producing rape proclivity has been well documented.

My own experiences in this area are the product of over twelve years of work with athletes and other men at Hobart College, where I have

*Dr. Berkowitz is Director, Counseling Center at Hobart and William Smith Colleges.

developed an innovative rape prevention program for men, and of my work as a consultant to athletic programs at numerous Ivy League and small private liberal arts colleges in the Northeast. In my workshops, I ask athletes to share phrases used by their coaches to describe team members who are not performing as expected. Coaches may use language which devalues women in order to motivate athletes to work harder and excel. The intent of such language runs counter to the fundamental assumptions underlying rape prevention education, serving to reinforce negative attitudes towards women that are associated with rape proclivity, and hindering men's ability to be empathic towards others.

Paradoxically, most men are uncomfortable with such language. In surveys I have conducted of men attending Ivy League and private liberal arts colleges in the Northeast, over 75% percent of the 100 respondents (including athletes) reported that they were bothered by the way men speak about women and sexuality when women are absent. Table 2 lists comments made by athletes in response to the question: "Briefly describe something that bothers you which men do when there are no women present." Few men express their discomfort with such behavior because of the widely held belief that most other men agree with and support it. When coaches themselves use language which devalues women and their bodies it becomes even less likely that athletes will express their discomfort. In addition, language which objectifies women's bodies and bragging about sexual exploits further reinforce men's beliefs that other men are much more sexually active then they really are. For example, surveys conducted at Hobart and William Smith Colleges indicate that men underestimate by a factor of ten the number of their peers who have not been sexually active in the last year. In these surveys, respondents were asked to report the amount of times they had intercourse in the last year and then estimate the frequency of intercourse among their peers. Forty-percent of the male students surveyed reported that they had not had intercourse in the last year, but those surveyed guessed that only 4% of their peers were sexually inactive in the past year.

These behaviors and perceptions — sexist and objectifying language used by peers to describe women, exaggerated beliefs regarding the sexual activity of other men, and derogatory references to women by coaches — all serve to reinforce and perpetuate those aspects of male culture which rape prevention programs are designed to weaken. Effective rape prevention programs for men should provide accurate information about men's attitudes, beliefs, and feelings about women, men's sexual activity, and sexual assault, as well as dispel the myth that all men support and engage in rape supportive attitudes and beliefs. Such programs can empower men who are silent in their discomfort with such behaviors to move out of the role of passive bystander into the role of confronting and reshaping behavior. Yet without the support and advocacy of coaches and athletic directors — often the most important individuals in the athletes life — such goals become unrealistic and unattainable. As one athlete commented: "Sometimes men talk about a girl that I respect and who is a good friend in such a way that degrades her. But this could be solved by just speaking up and telling the guy to shut up, but sometimes doing that can be more difficult that it sounds."

Effective rape prevention education with athletes thus begins with obtaining the support of athletic directors and coaches. The first step is to have all male coaches attend a rape prevention workshop. The opportunity to discuss openly, criticize, and react to a workshop will help create allies among the coaching staff. In addition, it will give coaches who are already supportive of our efforts the opportunity to speak out on our behalf. I am continually amazed and impressed by the sensitivity and support I have received from coaches who confound my own stereotypes about coaches and whose eyes have been opened by the experiences of significant women in their own lives — including female athletes. After securing the support of the athletic director and providing a demonstration workshop for coaches, the next step is to enlist the support of team captains and leaders by providing an opportunity for them to attend a workshop demonstration as well. Only then will we be in a position to provide programs for athletes with the likelihood that they will not be undermined and devalued by others who are important role models in their lives.

REFERENCES

Schaeffer, A.M. and E.S. Nelson. "Rape-supportive Attitudes: Effects of On-campus Residence and Education." *Journal of College Student Development.* 1993, 34:1275-179.

Lenihan, G.O., Rawlins, M.E., Eberly, C.G., Buckley, B. and B. Masters. "Gender Differences in Rape Supportive Attitudes Before and After a Date Rape Education Intervention." *Journal of College Student Development.* 1992, 33.331-338.

Berkowitz, A.D. "College Men as Perpetrators of Acquaintance Rape and Sexual Assault: A Review of Recent Research." *Journal of American College Health.* 1992, 40:175-181.

Berkowitz, A.D. "Rape Prevention for Men: Clinical and Education Program Strategies." Forthcoming in: *New Directions for Student Services Monograph Series.* Josey Bass, San Francisco, 1994.

Burt, M.R. "Rape Myths and Acquaintance Rape." In: Parrot, A., Bechhoffer, L. (Eds.). *Acquaintance Rape: The Hidden Crime.* New York: Wiley, 1991, p. 26-40.

Lundberg-Love, P. and R. Geffner. "Date Rape: Prevalance, Risk Factors and a Proposed Model." In: Pirog-Good, M.A. and J.E. Stets. *Violence in Dating Relationships: Emerging Social Issues.* New York: Praiger, 1989, Chapter 9.

A.B.

**Phrases Used by Coaches to Describe Athletes
Who Are Not Performing as Expected
(Selected Responses from Male Athletes)***

- Take your skirt off and get aggressive.

- You're playing like a bunch of sluts.

- You're playing like a bunch of girls.

- What are you, on the rag?

- What's wrong, does your pussy hurt?

- You're acting like a bunch of wimps.

- You don't deserve to be called men.

* Based on anonymous responses provided by athletes during rape prevention workshops.

Offensive Behaviors of Athletes in All-Male Groups*
(Selected Responses from Male Athletes)

- Talking about girls that they can't stand, but then acting like they are friends with them.

- When they talk about the sexual habits of girls that they know nothing about.

- Demands by friends to know how far sexually you've gone in a relationship.

- Bragging about sexual acts — giving details including names, positions, in a mocking way.

- Lying or exaggerating greatly the extent of sexual behavior.

- Asking how much play you got from a girl you hook-up with.

- Speaking about women as purely a means of pleasure and that is all.

- Talk about "taking advantage" of women.

- Talk about women in crude sexual terms.

- Talk about female anatomy.

- Guys like to talk about fooling around with girls and often, not always, talk about it with apparently no qualms. I tend to think fooling around is special and feel guilty, as if I had just betrayed that girl, when I reveal intimate moments.

* Subjects were asked to respond anonymously to the following question: "Briefly describe something that bothers you which men do when there are no women present."

OPENING THE PRESENTATION: CONNECT

When beginning a presentation, it is important to establish a rapport with the athletes. They are likely to feel threatened by the topic and thus by you. One way to ease this tension is by talking with them about their sport. It is therefore worthwhile to learn about the team ahead of time. If possible, attend one of the team's games or competitions prior to the presentation. If you are unfamiliar with the sport or the team, you can read newspaper reports or talk with someone who is knowledgeable. Then you can demonstrate your interest in the players by commenting on their athletic achievements.

Talk Sports, Tell Jokes

If the team is performing well, congratulate the athletes on a recent victory or their record during the previous season. Tell them that you appreciate their participation because you know that practices are long and leave them little free time. If you don't know a lot about sports, you can still show a basic interest without pretending to know more than you do. Ask them questions that allow them to tell you about themselves. Who are the teams to beat this year? When is their next home game? Are there many freshmen on the team, or do first-year students play on a junior varsity team?

Humor also can help diffuse anxiety at the outset of a presentation. Athletes enjoy laughing as a group and poking fun at each other. A facilitator's use of humor will depend on her or his personal style. Some people have a more natural ability to use humor than others: timing, and the way something is said, are as important as the words which are spoken. As an example, you could introduce yourself and say, "Today we're going to be talking about sex and power in relationships. Are there any authorities on sex here today? If you're too shy to raise your hand, we could have your friends identify you . . . Just kidding." Such a joke will likely elicit laughter and a barrage of nicknames directed at a few grinning team members. Without trivializing the seriousness of rape, joking with the players can provide an entree to the topic which helps lower defensiveness.

Incorporating sports jargon and metaphors into your presentation can also help you connect with the athletes. Though terms vary between sports and even schools, athletic culture has its own slang language. If sports language is not part of your vocabulary, find someone who speaks the local dialect and can offer some ideas. For example, a football team meeting is often called a "chalk talk." Usage in presentation: "We're here today to talk with you about sexual assault, which I realize is not a normal topic for a chalk talk." In sports which involve passing a ball (football, basketball, soccer, lacrosse), the following metaphor might apply: "If a woman says no, she's not open to your move. Pressuring her is like forcing a pass to a man whose not open. You wouldn't do that, right?"

A word of caution: while using humor and talking about sports can be an effective way of connecting with a team, it can also backfire. While its valuable to demonstrate an interest in the athletes, do not fake having knowledge of sports if you do not possess it. The athletes will see through your attempt. So if bantering about sports is not part of your repertoire, try to demonstrate an interest in them while presenting yourself honestly.

To determine which activities would be best, it is essential to get a "sense" of the group. Advance data gathering can help guide your plan, but you won't really know what will work with the group until you see how they respond to the first activity. Try to get group members to participate by using a non-threatening activity early in the session to which they can all relate. Non-threatening activities do not require telling intimate or personal things about yourself (like have you ever been involved in an acquaintance rape, and how do you feel about it?). Instead, they require non-personal information which is "safe" to share with others (such as have you ever seen a movie about acquaintance rape, and what was the main point of the movie?).

The opening activity should encourage communication about sex and allow you to assess whether the group is liberal or conservative, willing to participate honestly and openly, responsive to discussion or a more didactic approach. You should already have planned the logistics and should know about the obvious considerations (such as sex composition, age of group, etc.) by looking at the group. Upon completion of the initial activity, you should have most of the information you need to determine how to accomplish the objectives for the session. The first activity should allow for discussion and be provocative. Have a back up plan if the group does not respond to this type of activity.

Disclaimers

Most rape education programs for men emphasize the need to prevent becoming a perpetrator of the crime. However, some may have, themselves, been sexually victimized, either as children or young adults. This kind of programming could inadvertently be traumatic for some individuals who must listen to descriptions of circumstances similar to their own experiences. Therefore, some sort of statement regarding the reality that men are victimized too would validate some men's experiences. This can be done during the opening of the presentation. A mention of resources available to men who have been victimized would help those students who are still healing.

It would also be appropriate to mention at the outset that the issues to be discussed apply to same sex couples as well as heterosexual interactions. While athletic teams may have the reputation of being homophobic, there are still likely to be gay men on some teams. They should know that the information applies to their situations as well (although certainly gender roles exacerbate certain dynamics) because power inequities must be confronted in all relationships. Again, this statement can take place at the opening of a presentation or during any appropriate time in the discussion. However, it is important to consider whether this type of statement will be met with homophobic reactions at the beginning of a program, and whether that will influence the climate of the meeting. If you believe it would alienate a great many men at the beginning (and it is precisely those men you are most likely to want to reach), wait until the end of the program.

TECHNIQUES FOR ACHIEVING GOALS: EMOTIONAL AND COGNITIVE APPROACHES

Attitude change is much less difficult to achieve as a result of a one time program than behavior change. However, even attitude change is difficult. Educators must persuade men that 1) rape is devastating to the victim, and 2) attitudes which objectify women contribute to a social climate which fosters rape.

Lectures about statistics and facts will probably never accomplish these goals. However, using films, stories, or victim testimonials are more likely to make the participants feel emotional discomfort. The closer to their life experiences the emotional approach comes, the better. For example, they may not be able to relate to the pain a rape victim feels, but if you can help them see the vulnerability of their sisters, female friends, girlfriends, or mothers, by using a victim who shares some characteristics with the women in their lives, the participants may be more likely to relate.

Appeal to Empathy: Personalizing all Women

Men who rape depersonalize their victims. They are able to inflict pain and humiliation on women because they have a lack of concern for the woman's feelings. They experience their victims as objects. Therefore, a central goal of rape education for men is to foster empathy for women who are raped.

Some men have a limited capacity for empathy. Others may have sensitivity to a woman's experience, but it is overridden in certain situations by the influence of anger, alcohol, and peer pressure. Therefore a program should provide opportunities for men to experience vicariously the fear, pain, and shame that a woman feels from being raped. If the experience is sufficiently stirring, it has the potential for decreasing a man's proclivity to rape. Furthermore, it may motivate men to challenge exploitive attitudes and behaviors among their peers. *Chapter 7* describes activities and resources for fostering empathy.

A well told story can capture the imagination and evoke feelings in a unique way. Thus stories can powerfully illustrate a point or engage an audience at an emotional level. One kind of story is the testimonial: "When I was in college, I lived with a bunch of guys who made a hobby of harassing women. They used to. . ." For a male facilitator, this kind of story can foster credibility. As one athlete told a male facilitator after a presentation, "When you told those stories about your fraternity brothers, I said to myself, 'This guy has lived through what he's talking about.' "

A first-person testimonial also can be read aloud by a different person. For example, a facilitator can read a painful story written by a rape survivor. A third approach is to read a story written about another person or an incident. *I Never Called It Rape* by Robin Warshaw (1988, pp 122-123) contains an extremely moving passage which may be appropriate to read to a group. It tells the story of a young woman named Kathi who was assaulted by a group of athletes and then was ostracized at her high school for reporting the assault. Warshaw describes how Kathi became depressed and eventually killed herself. Reading this story can help men begin to understand the pain and long term consequences for a rape victim.

There are many survivors who are speaking out about their experiences. These testimonials, whether read, played on tape, or delivered in person are powerful in eliciting empathy from an audience. It is important to be sure that any survivor sharing her story in person is well-prepared ahead of time. It is inevitable that repeating a traumatic story in front of a group will cause strong feelings to emerge. Check with a counselor or therapist for the kinds of emotional preparation necessary for this type of testimonial. Discuss with the survivor the types of questions and comments she can anticipate, and plan how she might respond.

Many of the students may not know how to react to someone who has just shared something so personal. If the survivor is willing to answer questions from the audience, the facilitators may need to begin the questioning to warm up the group. It is possible the survivor may cry during her testimonial or have trouble sharing her story. Allow the emotions to flow. These presentations must be controlled by the survivor herself. Do not interrupt during her statement or begin speaking unless the survivor makes it clear that she would like you to help in some way, or that she is finished. It is critical that the survivor not be re-victimized by the experience.

Following a testimonial, encourage the athletes to talk about their feelings, rather than intellectualize or debate what was described. Draw the group's attention to the feelings revealed by player's statements and any subtleties in their comments that may need to be clarified.

Expect silence immediately following any testimonial. Most people need time to think about what they just saw or heard. Plan some gentle probes to bring out the audiences' thoughts and feelings. Following a videotaped testimony, ask the group to imagine that the young woman who they just watched is someone close to them, such as their sister or a friend.

Invoke the Law: The Legal Definition
And Consequences of Rape

Many incoming college students are at a relatively low level of moral development. In that case, they are likely to say that a man should not rape because it is against the law, and he could be put in jail. As a matter of fact Neil Malamuth (1981) asked college men anonymously if they would rape if they were assured of not getting caught. Thirty-one percent said yes. Although rape law differs from state to state, there are some similarities. Rape is generally defined as sexual intercourse against a victim's will and without his or her consent, or if force, violence, threat of force, or threat of violence is used by the assailant to gain compliance, or if the victim has sexual intercourse while he or she was fearful for his or her safety or life, or if the victim was unable to give consent (by reason of being passed out, blacked out, asleep, or mentally incompetent).

This last condition is most important to explain because many people believe that if a woman gets drunk then she deserves what happens to her. But the law differs in it's interpretation on this matter. If she can't give informed consent, it is rape. In many states, if a woman gets herself drunk she cannot charge a man with rape as long as she is able to give informed consent. However, once she passes out, regardless of how she got drunk, she is no longer able to give informed consent. Sex under the latter condition is legally considered rape.

Male athletes also need to be made aware of the fact that a woman does not even need to verbalize "no" for forced sexual intercourse to be considered rape. If a woman is so fearful for her safety or life that she believes that if she says no that she will be harmed or killed, the act is still rape. For example, if a woman is with a powerful male athlete of an aggressive sport and she thinks he will become violent with her if she refuses sexual intercourse because he is drunk, the law calls that rape too. So the only way men can really know that they are having sex with a willing partner is to ask and get positive verbal consent. Failing to do so may result in a criminal conviction and possible jail time.

Teach Social Skills:
Words to Use with Sexual Partners

In addition to changing attitudes about sexual assault, educators must provide men with specific social skills which they can use to change their behavior. One important social skill is language. Learning new language skills not only improves communication, it can reshape the way men think about women. For example, by learning to ask, "Do you want me inside of you?" before penetrating a woman, the man elicits the answer he needs. But of equal importance is he reminds himself that his sexual partner has a right to say yes or no.

Many men have difficulty talking with their partners during a sexual encounter. A good discussion question is to ask them why it is hard to communicate effectively. One problem is that they don't know how to talk about sex without seeming awkward. Another obstacle is that they may feel it is not "manly" to talk seriously about sexual desires. Both of these problems can be overcome with the help of the group. Request from the group ways to ask a woman what she wants sexually in a manner that doesn't spoil spontaneity. There will probably be at least a few men who can provide you with appropriate responses. By eliciting the ideas from the group, the men will model for each other how and what to say. Although answers from peers are the most credible, be prepared to offer your own suggestions and ask them to judge them.

Use Positive Peer Pressure

A difficult challenge is teaching men ways to criticize other men whose language or behavior is exploitive of women. They may not recognize that a peer is being exploitive, and even if they do, most men do not know how to intervene. They usually fear confrontation and rejection by the group. By discussing ways to confront one another's behavior, the group increases the acceptability of criticism.

The first step is to reach some consensus (the group rarely will reach full consensus) about what kinds of behaviors constitute exploitation. This is an important process, since the group has an opportunity to publicly define the norms of acceptable behavior. The group may be able to cite examples, but be prepared with some of your own. You should be able to point out behaviors that the group previously had not considered exploitive. Offering your examples can be tricky since many men might disagree with your opinion. The classic response to an example of exploitation is, "Oh, that's just guys having fun. No one is hurt by that." When faced with this attitude, ask the group for opposing opinions before responding with your own view.

Generally in a group of this nature, someone will make a sexist or mysoginistic remark. The more inappropriate the remark, the more likely another team member will be to criticize or oppose the speaker and offer a more reasonable point of view. There are likely to be men in the group who have girlfriends, friends or sisters who have been raped, and so they understand the impact of rape better than most men. If one member of the team says, "If she comes up to my room, and she is drunk, she deserves sex, whether she wants it or not," one of his team mates is likely to say, "The only time she deserves sex is if she asks for it. Hey man, would you feel that way if some guy said that about your little sister?" It is better to allow them to confront each other and to model desired behavior than for us to tell them the "correct" answers. Peer pressure is much more effective than an expert giving advice.

One technique for working toward a consensus is to build on the most appropriate responses the group offers to an example of exploitation. Some men will dismiss a given example as harmless, while others will disagree. For example: "A group of men sit on the porch of their fraternity house drinking beer. As women pass by on the sidewalk, the men shout insults at them, calling them whores, dykes, and bitches." Ask the athletes for their opinions of the situation. Solicit a range of viewpoints, but guide the discussion so that the men who find the behavior degrading have ample opportunity to express their view and to critique those with differing viewpoints.

Other examples of exploitive behaviors which directly harm women or contribute to a rape culture include the following:

- spiking women's drinks at a party;

- men disrobing while dancing at a party;

- displaying posters of nude women or posters that objectify women's bodies;

- wet t-shirt contests;

- advertising parties with themes that are degrading to women.

If the group can reach at least a partial consensus that a particular behavior is exploitive, then you can begin exploring ways to respond. Below are a few examples of responses men can use to an exploitive comment. Ask the athletes to generate their own list and evaluate the options you suggest.

Incident: During dinner at his fraternity, Bill makes a comment about a woman he met at a party who refused to go to bed with him: "I think that she's a cockteaser and deserves to be f---ed."

If the players do not view this as offensive, you might add that the fraternity is on probation because of a sexual harassment charge involving Bill.

Possible responses from his friends, in descending order of confrontation:

- "Bill, you're an a--hole." (criticism of character; risky if Bill is well-respected)

- "That's a stupid thing to say." (confrontational, but directed at the comment rather than the character of the individual)

- "Am I the only guy here who thinks that that was a ridiculous thing to say?" (invoking disapproval from the group.)

- "Oh, that's really a good idea, Bill." (spoken sarcastically)

- "What in the world do you mean by that?" (incredulity, opens the door for dialogue, be prepared to respond further)

- "I can't believe you said that" or "You've got to be kidding." (incredulity)

- "Yeah, Bill, we ought to go out and rape all the women who don't want to sleep with you." (mocking confrontation)

- "That's sick." (not directed at Bill, mumbled while looking down at one's meal)

- "Bill, your language reflects an insensitivity to the feelings and rights of women." (too sensitive, liberated man's response that will be laughed out of the room)

- Give a disapproving look. (nonverbal disapproval)

- Silence. (tacit approval)

Another technique is to use a fun approach to skillbuilding. The activity in *Appendix K* is a good example of ways to get athletes involved in making decisions together about acceptable responses, peer involvement and developing desirable skills.

Dispel Sexual Myths

Ignorance about basic sexual functioning can reinforce distorted attitudes about sexual rights and needs. Clarifying a few basic concepts about male sexuality can challenge ideas that men may use as rationalizations for abusive behavior. Men frequently ask questions which invite you to dispel basic myths (e.g., all men are sexually active or men always want to have sexual intercourse). If the group does not raise these points, weave them into the presentation yourself.

1) **Masturbation:** Some men feel that sex with a woman is the only way to release sexual tension. They are entitled to that belief. But if such a belief motivates the individual to try and "score," it may help to suggest an alternative: masturbation. While many men masturbate, some view it as immoral or undesirable. While respecting the opinion of those who do not masturbate, it is helpful to clarify some facts: masturbation does not make one homosexual, does not make a person anti-social and does not have harmful physical consequences. Nor does it make one "less of a man." Explain that the majority of men masturbate at some time and that it can provide an outlet for sexual tension. As exemplified by the following exchange between two athletes, the range of awareness and experience with masturbation can be quite wide:

    Athlete #1: "Have any of you guys ever masturbated? I did it once."

    Athlete #2: "Once? Are you kidding? I'm lucky the thing hasn't fallen off by now."

2) **Blue Balls:** When a male becomes sexually aroused but does not reach orgasm, the unreleased tension in his genitals can produce an aching sensation known to many adolescents as "blue balls." The potential for blue balls is sometimes used by

young men as a justification for pressuring their partners to have sex. Just because they have blue balls does not give them the right to have sex. Remind them that the ache is just an ache: "no one has ever died from blue balls." Moreover, the tension can be alleviated through masturbation or it will dissipate over time.

3) **The point of no return:** A young man once articulately explained to a group that rape is never justified. Nevertheless, he added one caveat: "A woman always has the right to say no, unless they are in bed and he is so turned on that he can't stop." The idea that a man can "lose control of himself" is one of the most persistent and pernicious myths about male sexuality. As one rapist told his victim after raping her, "I'm sorry, I know it was wrong, but I couldn't stop myself." The fact is that there is never a point at which a man loses control. Illustrate this point with the following example: "Let's say you are over at your girlfriends' house while her parents are out. The two of you decide to have sex. You get into bed, become wildly aroused, and are just about to penetrate her when her parents show up and call out, "Hi, we're home." Would you be able to stop? Of course you would.

THINKING ON YOUR FEET

Diffusing Tension

Undoubtedly, people will be tense at the start of any program if they know it is about sexual assault. Therefore, you may want to keep the true purpose of the program confidential (see *Chapter 5* for specific suggestions). If the audience knows the topic, you may want to use humor at the start to help discharge tension and reduce defensiveness. The humor should not be at the expense of any groups, and never be homophobic, racist, sexist, etc.

If the facilitators can join in making fun of dating and sexuality expectations, the serious statements regarding rape prevention will, in contrast, carry more weight. It is acceptable and even desirable to allow the players to enjoy themselves at the start of the program, to begin to feel comfortable with the facilitators. The audience will be more open if the facilitators appear genuine and relaxed. It will be most effective in helping them see the dysfunction of their current patterns or behavior, and how and why to change them.

Be prepared for some degree of rowdiness and/or crudeness. Talking about sexual encounters in a large group can generate bursts of laughter and rapid-fire comments, usually as a result of nervousness or anxiety. Do not shy away from repeating any graphic language they may use or asking them to define terms that may be unfamiliar to you. If the group senses the least bit of discomfort or unwillingness to join in some of the fun (within limits of course), they may take advantage of the opportunity to make you squirm and will be less cooperative when you need their full attention.

Responding Non-defensively to Challenges and Sexist Remarks

Even though sexist remarks may irritate and frustrate educators, if men are to gain a better understanding of these issues we must allow them to say what they are really thinking. It is the educator's job to help men who make sexist remarks to see why that point of view is wrong and possibly dangerous. If someone makes an inappropriate remark, you may want to ask, "Does anyone want to respond to that?" and let the challenge come from a peer of the speaker.

If a participant is making fun of the program, or is making derogatory comments which the other athletes laugh at, the facilitator may be able to redirect the group by saying something like, "What's the joke? I don't understand." The person who made the comment will have to take responsibility for the comment or stop being disruptive. If the comment is explained, then the facilitator can use that comment as a "teachable moment" to discuss the possibly inappropriate, sexist, or mysoginist comment.

One effective facilitation strategy is for the group leader to frame questions so that the "right information of opinions" comes from the group. This way, peer education can evolve and it prevents the facilitator from having to preach to the group.

Handling Hostile Groups

We believe that the best approach to handling hostile groups is to remain non-defensive. If they want to challenge the female facilitator because they believe she is a feminist, it is best for the male facilitator to deflect the attack and discuss the issue in terms of how men can work together to alleviate the problem, rather than getting angry at the messenger. In addition, try to diffuse angry groups at the beginning by telling them that you are there as their ally and to help them have a better college experience, not to accuse or blame them.

If they become hostile, you can deal with the hostility directly, with humor, or by putting it off to be discussed later individually. For example, you could say "That is an interesting point but it is not exactly related to the topic of this exercise. If you would like to discuss it further, lets talk after the program." Once, when doing a program in which we asked for questions from the audience on 3x5 cards, one card was returned from the group which read, "It is so hot in here, why don't we all take our clothes off and get naked?". One facilitator responded to the message by saying "I am perfectly comfortable, but if whoever wrote this card would like to take his clothes off, feel free." Everyone laughed and the tension was over.

The facilitator needs to select an approach which works best for him or her, but becoming defensive seems to defeat the goals of the program.

Predictable Questions and Good Responses

During the program, facilitators want to encourage questions from the audience as much as possible. This is often the most important part of any discussion because it affords the opportunity to air concerns so the whole group hears them. A good way to respond initially to a question, however offensive it may strike you, is to say something like, "That's a good question," "Thank you for asking that," "I'm glad you asked that," or "I'm often asked that question." This approach shows respect for the individual and may help diffuse an attack on you which is embedded in the question. The fact is that even offensive questions are good questions for the purpose of education. Prepare yourself for comments and questions which may elicit negative emotions in you and try to welcome them as opportunities to teach.

Typical questions you might encounter are:

- If she doesn't say no (because she is scared of me or afraid of how I might react if she resists) and we have sex . . . can she call that rape? (yes) Then, how do I know if she wants to have sex or not?

- **A:** Ask her . . . you can check with her by saying "Is this okay for you?"

- **Q:** When does "no" really mean "no" in a sexual situation?

- **A:** Communication is affected by more than verbals; body language, facial expression and tone of voice all play a part. It is your responsibility to pay attention to all of these things, rather than assuming she doesn't mean it. If she is pulling away and looks distraught, it's a pretty good sign she means it!

- **Q:** What exactly does "no" really mean in a sexual situation?

- **A:** That is one thing you need to find out. Does it mean no to every sexual activity, just intercourse, oral sex, etc. You will have to ask along the way.

- **Q:** What exactly does the law say rape is?

- **A:** Although the law changes from state to state, in general, forced sexual intercourse without consent is rape. In New York, there are additional conditions that may constitute rape such as . . . (See *Chapter 6* for the legal definition in New York State or include the legal definition from your state if other than New York.)

- **Q:** What if we have sex and then she changes her mind the next morning?

- **A:** This will not be an issue if you are sure she wanted to be involved in the sexual activity at the time it occurred. It is your responsibility to be sure that whatever you engage in is consensual — how do you do that again? This is many men's worst fear, but it rarely occurs. The rate of false reports of rape is similar to false reports of other crimes (about 2%). It is far more likely that a woman will be raped and never report it.

- **Q:** What if I was really drunk and didn't really know what I was doing?

- **A:** According to the law, "liquor courage" is no excuse for unconsensual sexual intercourse. You cannot be exonerated from a rape charge because you were drunk.

- **Q:** Don't some women say "no" just because they don't want to seem too easy?

- **A:** Sometimes. But the man has to assume she means no. If she means "yes" she'll let him know after he stops.

- **Q:** If both the man and the woman are drunk, is the man responsible for what happens?

- **A:** Having been intoxicated is not a legal defense for a man. Moreover, a woman is unable to give legal consent if she is incapacitated by alcohol. If they are both drunk almost to the point of being blacked out and sexual intercourse occurs, the one who was the aggressor is legally at fault. It is most important to remember that if a woman can't give informed consent, it is rape. In many states, if a woman gets herself drunk she cannot charge a man with rape as long as she is able to give informed consent. However, once she passes out, regardless of how she got drunk, she is no longer able to give informed consent. Sex under the latter condition is legally considered rape.

- **Q:** If she says "no" when he's about to penetrate her, the guy might not be able to stop.

- **A:** There is no physiological point at which a man can't stop himself. If her mother walked in, he'd stop.

- **Q:** If she gets into bed and then changes her mind, its partly her fault if she gets raped.

- **A:** Rape is always the fault of the perpetrator, never the victim. She may have used bad judgement leading him on, but that doesn't mean she deserves to be raped. The man may have a right to be angry, but never to harm the woman.

- **Q:** Why is all the focus on men. Can't a woman sexually abuse/harass a guy?

- **A:** Yes, women can sexually exploit men. And doing so is just as wrong as it is for a man to exploit a women. However, the power differences between men and women make violence towards women much more frequent and usually more severe. The law allows for either men or women to be assailants and/or victims.

Providing Useful Handouts

It is very important to send the audience home with some written material on acquaintance rape, prevention strategies, and resources available in the community because they may not have heard all of the important points of the program and may want to know more about the issue. Handouts are best given to the audience when they leave, unless facilitators plan to use them specifically to support part of the discussion. In that case, hand out only those appropriate to the discussion at the time. It is best not to have handouts available when students enter, because they will be reading them rather than participating fully in the program. If there are several handouts, and your budget supports it, print each on a different color paper. They are more appealing and are easier to refer to than many sheets all on white. See the appendices for some handout suggestions.

Conducting Formal Evaluation

Some type of evaluation of these programs is crucial. Knowledge and attitude changes of the participants can be measured by administering pre- and post-tests, such as the *Attitudes Towards Women Scale* (Spence & Helmrich, 1972), the *HyperMasculinity Scale* (Mosher, 1986), or the proclivity to *Rape Scale* (Malamuth, 1981). Alternatively, pre- and post-tests can be developed to make them most applicable to your needs, goals and interests. Post measures can be conducted immediately after the program, and/or some later period (such as the end of the season or school year). Behavior change is more difficult to assess, but may be measured pre/post longitudinally. Graduate students looking for thesis topics may be intrigued by an opportunity to evaluate this kind of program.

You also want to collect less formal evaluation information in order to revise and shape future programs. Questions such as "the best part of the session was . . .", "the most important thing I learned was . . . ," etc. will provide useful feedback.

In any event, evaluation should always reflect the issues presented in your program. Generic evaluations or scales may not provide you with the information that would be most useful.

CHOOSING ACTIVITIES:
A GAME PLAN APPROACH

Since all groups differ, the Game Plan Approach is recommended. It assumes that the goals and objectives for most groups are the same, but the ways to accomplish these will differ. This chapter outlines activities as they relate to ten major programming goals.

No session will even begin to be effective in accomplishing goals and objectives unless the group is willing to confront difficult issues. In the case of athletes, there may be resistance. But although a group usually needs substantial time to develop cohesion and a sense of trust, athletes are already a team and may adjust to the challenge quickly. The key to keeping the athletes interested is to change the pace, pattern, and focus of the activities.

Educational programs should be designed to empower participants to avoid acquaintance rape by helping them understand the dysfunctional aspects of peer pressure, sex stereotypic behaviors, and drug and alcohol use plus giving them realistic alternative means of interacting with others. Improvisational, interactive theater works well in presenting these messages in an interesting and realistic way. Making the scenes situation-specific, such as having the man be an athlete and using a typical athlete's party as the setting, could be most effective.

One model using interactive theater as the central element of the new student orientation acquaintance rape prevention program used at Cornell University follows.

Students watch three scenarios presented by actors; the first two start the same way. In the first scene both the man and the woman on the "date" behave in a sex stereotypic and intoxicated manner and a rape results. The audience then discusses with the actors the dynamics of the situation to point to the dysfunction of their behaviors. The actors remain in character during the discussion. Audience members are encouraged to make suggestions to the actors to help them avoid involvement in acquaintance rape in the future.

Then the actors enact the same scene again, but this time the actors incorporate the suggestions made by the audience (and modified by the facilitators if necessary). The end result is that there is no rape in the

CHAPTER 7

second scene, and the characters like each other better at the end of the scenario. The man listens to the woman, asks what she wants sexually and admits his own vulnerabilities; the woman is more assertive, communicative and self-assured. Both partners act more maturely and responsibly, but there is still room for improvement. Since the actors incorporate ideas that the audience generated, students can see how the suggestions work and are more likely to carry them out, than if the suggestions had been made by the facilitators.

An alternative second scene is appropriate for more sophisticated and advanced groups. In this scene, set at dinner before the party, the actors actually discuss the advantages and disadvantages of having sex, and the dysfunctions of peer pressure and alcohol use. They consequently decide to not have sex that night, and to limit their alcohol use. Both partners act responsibly in the alternate second scene.

The depictions in the scenes are realistic and should be specific to the audience. The result of this approach is that the audience members are able to see how behavior change could result in more positive dating outcomes (Parrot and Bechhofer, 1991).

EXPLORE SEXUAL ENTITLEMENT AND POWER

Because men's sexual entitlement is a fundamental part of a patriarchal culture, it is an inherent part of the rape problem. It contributes to the cultural misunderstandings and victim-blaming attitudes commonly associated with the problem of rape. Rape education should include some activity to help men identify their attitudes regarding sexual entitlement. Here are some suggestions:

1)   As the students arrive for a program, give each individual a sheet with two incomplete sentences pre-printed on each page. Tell them not to put their names on the sheet and ask them to complete the sentences individually without input from their teammates. Give them just a few minutes to complete the task. Collect the sheets after everyone is finished.

While one facilitator is leading an "icebreaker" or other activity, the other should review the sheets. Choose a few responses that are funny, thoughtful, and responsible, plus some that identify rape-supportive beliefs, sexual entitlement, or are troubling. Read each of the chosen responses aloud and ask the group what they think. Encourage as many audience members to respond as possible as a way to assure that a variety of opinions are heard.

Suggestions for incomplete sentences are:

- "I feel someone is giving me a sexual come-on when . . ."

- "A man is owed sex when . . ."

- "I feel manipulated in a dating situation when . . ."

- "Cues from my date which make me wary are . . ."

- "When a woman sends me conflicting messages where her behavior says yes and her words say no, I believe . . ."

- "When beginning a relationship, I want . . ."

More ideas are provided in *Appendix F.*

Once the facilitators have allowed the men to air their feelings about the answers, they must be sure that the rape-supportive attitudes were clearly identified as such. While it is important to let the students give their opinions, it is more important to pay close attention to apparent attitudes or stereotyped beliefs that can lead to sexual assault and to focus on them when they arise. In some instances, the men themselves may not provide any input to critique or question answers that are clearly incorrect in their assumptions. The discussion can become rowdy and important educable moments can easily slip away with the distraction of many voices. The men must not leave the program believing that responses such as "a man is owed sex . . . when he pays for a date's meal" is in any way a safe or correct assumption.

2)   Show a video or vignette that depicts a rape scene. Leave lots of time for discussion. Be sure to include trick questions for the audience such as "What kind of thing could a woman do that would make her deserve to be raped?" These will help bring out any attitudes that need to be addressed.

3)   Give the men a questionnaire to complete, such as the one from a UCLA study (Goodchilds, et al., 1988). Then use it as a tool to

discuss issues such as: "Under what circumstances is it okay to force sex?" You may want to collect them afterwards to have a good summary of the student's attitudes that came into the program. Hopefully they change some after the discussions.

4) Read a testimony from a self-described rapist such as "Seven Years Ago" (Jack M.,1992). Discuss the rapists attitude and power over his victim.

5) There are mainstream videos available that have depictions of rape in them. These can be used as triggers for discussion. "Thelma & Louise," "The Accused" and "Pretty Woman" all have scenes that are particularly good triggers for discussions about sexual entitlement and power dynamics.

6) Lead a discussion about what to do when "you don't get what you want sexually." Alternatives (such as masturbation) for men who feel stimulated and then find themselves without a release because a partner says no may be met with unbelieving laughter but the discussion can lead to validating their feelings. Explain that it is acceptable and understandable to be angry or frustrated but not okay to use force or violence.

Connection Between Attitudes and Rape

Because rape and assault are intricately connected to values, attitudes, and less threatening but still harmful behaviors, the sexual violence progression in *Chapter 4* can be shown to an audience to help them understand the relationships. Other activities that focus on the connection between certain cultural attitudes and rape include:

1) Revisit a rapist's testimony and examine his descriptions of his beliefs and how they led him to commit rape.

2) Use a victim's description of an assault (either written, video or live) to lead a discussion about the incident and how the attitudes of the perpetrator contributed to the assault. The Santa Monica Rape Treatment Center's *Campus Rape* film has several victims describing assaults. The Santa Monica Rape Treatment Center's *She's Only Sixteen* public service announcement specifically addresses "he wouldn't take no for an answer."

The story of "Kathi" in Robin Warshaw's *I Never Called It Rape* would also be a good trigger (Warshaw, 1988, p. 122-123).

3) Personalize the connection. At the beginning of the program give each of the men a 3x5 card and a pencil. Ask them to write down the names of the six women to whom they are closest. They can be their girlfriends, mothers, sisters, friends, etc. Ask them to set the card aside and go on with the program. When you are ready to address this issue, ask them to look at the card with the list of names and to visualize those women in their lives. Then tell them that the statistics estimate that 1 in 6 women will be sexually assaulted. Explain that 1 in 3 girls are estimated to be sexually abused as children (Finkelhor, et al., 1990). Therefore, there is a likelihood that one of the women on their list will be or already has been the victim of sexual assault. Process the activity by asking how that makes them feel. A good conclusion would be to lead a discussion about how to react if someone confides that they or someone they know has been abused, what to say and most importantly what not to say, what the local resources are, etc.

An alternative would be to ask the men to think of 11 male friends, teammates, brothers or whomever. It is estimated that 1 in 11 men are at risk of committing sexual assault. Ask the men to think about the kinds of messages those men get that rape or sexual assault is sometimes justified. Ask them to think about what those men's lives would be like if they were accused or convicted or rape. Then have a follow up discussion about what the individuals could do to intervene to prevent sexual assault.

5) Examine how culture promotes rape (the affective component).

Sexual violence is learned. In a patriarchal society, males learn early that they hold more power than females. Furthermore, the media often teaches that men are entitled to sex and that violence against women is acceptable. Unfortunately, such messages are so ubiquitous and normative that most people fail to recognize them or their connection to rape. Examining these images out of context can help men see their destructive effect. On the other hand, the media also educates the public about the impact of rape. Two effective methods for presenting these various images are slides and videos.

Slides

To underscore the impact of rape on society, show slides of news articles and magazine cover stories on rape. Popular magazines such as *Newsweek, Time* and the *New York Times Magazine Section* have run several cover stories in recent years, and libraries may have back issues available. Images of athletes such as Mike Tyson in prison can be particularly effective. In addition, the Santa Monica Rape Crisis Center has a series of educational posters which make excellent slides.

Images which promote sexual violence abound in magazine advertisements and novelty shops such as Spencer Gifts. Some send indirect messages, such as beer advertisements portraying scantily clad women serving men. Sexually oriented greeting cards may reinforce dangerous ideas, such as one which shows a woman on the cover saying, "No, no, no!." On the inside the card reads, "Well, maybe." There also are bumper stickers and buttons with messages such as, "If I don't get laid soon, someone is going to get hurt." Many sexually explicit posters objectify women and send blunt messages to men about sexual entitlement. One shows two women in revealing clothes with bags over their heads. The message printed at the bottom reads, "The late night environmental dilemma: paper or plastic?" Choose and present such images carefully: men may find them erotic and fail to recognize their exploitive function.

Video

Dreamworlds by Jhally from the Communications Department at the University of Massachusetts at Amherst is a collection of video clips from MTV which portray or promote acts of sexual aggression. Also, several popular films on video contain scenes which condone sexual violence. In *Gone With the Wind,* Rhett Butler grabs Scarlett O'Hara and drags her off to bed as she struggles to resist him. The following scene shows her lying blissfully in bed the next morning. In the final episode of the hit television series *Moonlighting,* Maddie and David get into a fight. After they hit each other, David grabs Maddie, kisses her, and then drags her onto the floor where they make love. The message to men in these two scenes is that women really want sex, especially when you rough them up a little. In the movie *Henry and June,* June is raped by a stranger wearing a mask. The film shows her beginning to enjoy the rape. After she shows pleasure, the rapist reveals himself as her husband.

Explore Power of Group Behavior

Because of the connection between "groupthink" and gang rape, and because athletes are most frequently members of a team, educators may want to examine the dynamics of group behavior. "'Groupthink' occurs when a group arrives at a premature decision consensus that overlooks or excludes important aspects of the situation or the group" (Janis, 1972). Facilitators can lead a discussion on what it means to be a member of their team. Ask them to outline why they enjoy the team work, the spirit, the loyalty and the camaraderie. Then ask them to list the disadvantages of being on a team. This will probably be a less enthusiastic brainstorm, because of the peer pressure in the room. Facilitators can point out some of the things a man might do as part of a group that he would not do individually, and then lead the discussion into the types of dynamics that lead to gang rape.

A highly effective trigger for a discussion about group behavior is, again, the use of videos. Films such as *Casualties of War*, *The Accused* and *School Daze* provide striking visual images to start discussion about the nuts and bolts of "groupthink."

Examine the Scope of the Problem

At some point during a program, facilitators want to be sure to provide the men with an understanding of the scope of the problem of rape and violence against women. With rape being the most underreported crime, it is possible some men may not believe there is any problem. While lecture format is strongly advised against for these programs, you may need to plan on a mini-lecture that will quickly and effectively offer information about the extent of the crime. Develop a quiz game that asks the men themselves to predict the statistics, review them, and correct any misinformation. Try to use current events to illustrate your points. Read excerpts from *Against Our Will* by Susan Brownmiller, or reports from countries engaged in war (in 1993, reports on the rape epidemic in war-torn Bosnia were prevalent news items, *MS. Magazine* carried victim testimonials). Develop a slide show that depicts historical changes in rape reports and their media coverage during the last decade. Collect TV news items and splice them together to make a video that describes the statistics. In any of these formats, be sure to include related issues such as the connection between alcohol abuse and sexual assault.

Teach the Law and Its Consequences

The definition of the law is available in *Chapter 6*. However, there are often questions asked regarding the legal definition which bear repeating here.

- **Q:** Why are men punished for what they do when they are drunk, but women are not?

- **A:** In most states the law is gender neutral. This means that either a man or a woman may be the victim of the perpetrator of rape. If a woman was drunk and was the one doing the forcing, she could be arrested for rape. In reality, in this, and most other cultures, men are much more likely to be aggressive than women, so in most cases the man is doing the forcing.

- **Q:** If a woman doesn't even have to say no to sex for it to be rape, how can I know if I am raping her?

- **A:** Ask her if she wants to have sex with you in a place and way that would allow her to say no without feeling threatened.

- **Q:** If sexual intercourse is the only behavior that is included in rape, what about other things like oral sex?

- **A:** Any forced sexual behavior is against the law. However, other types of offenses are usually considered sodomy or deviate sexual intercourse. They are also felonies. (This answer may vary from state to state.)

We may be able to create fear of arrest and conviction in these men by presenting the idea that they may go to jail for having sex with an unwilling partner and by citing examples with which they can relate (such as Mike Tyson, the football players from Glen Ridge, N.J. or a local case). Even if they are not successfully prosecuted, if they are charged it will cost them considerable money to defend themselves, and they are likely to have a tarnished or questionable reputation from that time forward. Consider the cases of William Kennedy Smith and Justice Clarence Thomas. Both of these men are likely to be remembered for the accusations against them of rape and sexual harassment, respectively, for the remainder of their lives. Some people will always wonder if, although exonerated, they were really guilty. In addition, defending oneself against such a charge may cost the alleged assailant some time away from college, a possible sanction by their school through an administrative process, and he may also be sued civilly instead of, or in addition to, the criminal charge. Even if a man is successful in defending himself against a criminal charge, he may be found guilty in a campus judicial system because the standard of proof is usually less stringent on a campus.

Challenge Victim Blaming

In any rape education program, victim blaming statements will be made; some subtle, some blatant. The most egregious need to be challenged, but you may want to "pick your battles," especially with a hostile audience. The tone with which they are challenged is also important. It is best left up to the group to challenge each other. If someone makes a victim blaming comment, facilitators might want to first ask if anyone in the group would like to respond. Here, use peer pressure to educate. If that doesn't solicit any response, use tact when responding. Keep in mind that if the men feel attacked, they will shut down and the educational opportunity will be lost. Try to point out the origins of the statements. For example, if someone says that a woman who was raped was a "tease," point out the cultural limits placed upon women's sexuality.

Link the discussion with men's sexual entitlement and power in society. Ask them what you call a man who "scores" a lot (stud) and what you call a woman who has multiple sexual partners (slut) and have a discussion on why. If someone suggests clothing, attitude or behavior was responsible for an assault, discuss the responsibility placed on women not to be in the wrong place at the wrong time. Then use stories, anecdotes or statistics that refute the assumptions. Interactive theater is particularly effective in addressing this issue. Audience members able to interact with actors in role playing frequently will ask a female portraying a victim why they went to the man's room, why they drank so much. To hear the woman respond and tell them what she was thinking challenges intellectualization and helps the audience understand the rationale for motives.

A dialogue that describes a man being cross-examined after he was robbed is an excellent tool for addressing victim blaming remarks and their origins. Clearly point out the assumptions about behavior unfairly bestowed upon women when a rape occurs.

While any and all victim blaming remarks must be addressed, do not dwell on them. They can easily swell into lengthy discussions and distract from the rest of the program. Strategize how to respond and move on.

Generate Recommendations for Behavior Change

1)   Strategies for preventing sexual assault

If time allows, help the team to list behaviors they can use to reduce the risk of sexual assault. Include sexual behaviors as well as indirect activities such as drinking. If time is short or if the group does not generate the answers you desire, simply list a few main practices such as the following:

- When a woman says "no," stop and talk. Assume "no" means "no," not "maybe."

- Don't mistake silence for consent. Fear can cause silence.

- Don't pressure other guys to drink or have sex.

- Challenge and criticize other guys when they harass or degrade women.

- Treat all women with respect and dignity.

- Remember that the sexual control center is located above the shoulders, not between the legs.

See *Appendix N* for a more extensive list. Distribute copies of the list to the athletes at the end of the presentation.

2)   Responding to victims

Remind the athletes that it is likely that someone they know and care about has or will be sexually assaulted. How friends respond to a disclosure of sexual assault can affect the woman's recovery. Therefore, instruct the athletes on the do's and don'ts of helping someone who has been assaulted:

Do

- . . . believe your friend. people rarely lie about rape or assault.

- . . . listen to your friend and concentrate on understanding her or his feelings.

- . . . allow your friend to be silent; you don't have to talk every time she or he stops talking.

- . . . let your friend know that you understand her or his feelings. For example, you might say, "You must have been very frightened."

- . . . ask how you can help,

- . . . offer to accompany your friend in seeking medical attention or counseling or in going to the police.

- . . . help your friend regain a sense of control. Support her or him in making decisions about whom to tell and how to proceed.

- . . . remind your friend that rape is the rapist's fault, not the victims.

- . . . offer shelter or companionship so that your friend doesn't have to be alone.

- . . . help your friend learn about, recognize and seek treatment for signs of rape trauma syndrome.

Don't

- . . . ask questions that imply that the rape was your friend's fault, such as "Why did you go to his room?" "Why didn't you scream?" "Why didn't you run away?"

- . . . touch or hug your friend unless you're sure your friend is comfortable with physical contact.

- . . . act in ways that are upsetting to your friend. Be wary of phrases like "If I could find the creep, I'd kill him." Although you may be trying to be supportive, that type of comment may simply add to your friend's burden. While anger is a normal response, taking the law into one's own hands creates even more problems. Moreover, retribution may be against the victim's wishes.

- . . . tell anyone about the assault without your friend's permission.

- . . . tell your friend what to do; rather, help her or him explore the options. Among the complex decisions your friend will have to make are whether to report the assault to the police and whether to press charges. You may be able to suggest resource people who can be helpful in discussing the options, such as the local rape crisis organization (Cornell Advocates for Rape Education, 1989).

See *Appendix M.*

3)   Parting words

Offer a few messages about men as victims, particularly because there probably will be survivors of child sexual abuse present.

- Men can be victims of sexual abuse as well as women. The FBI reports that ten percent of all reported sexual assaults are committed against males. Many men (estimates are 1 in 9) were abused as children.

- Unwanted sexual contact can come from anyone, at any time in your life, even family members.

- Sexual abuse does not always leave bruises or involve overt violence. Sometimes force occurs as threats or coercion.

- If you have been sexually assaulted, it is not your fault. The blame for sexual abuse lies entirely with the perpetrator.

- If you feel confused about a sexual experience, tell someone you trust. Keep telling until someone helps you.

Finally, as you end the presentation:

- Thank the athletes for their time and participation.

- Wish them luck on their season.

- Ask them to take the handouts home, read them, and share them with others.

APPENDIX A
DISCUSSION INTRODUCTIONS

■ Objective: To introduce the sexual assault issues in a non-threatening manner and to prepare the audience to discuss the topic

■ Time: 15 minutes

■ Materials needed: None

Directions to facilitator:

Tell the group what the program is about including what is on the agenda. In particular, mention that the time will not be spent in lecture, and that the discussion relies on audience participation. Emphasize the fact that you recognize they are student leaders and have particular issues and pressures as athletes at the school. Choose one or several of the questions below to begin discussion. Once several audience members have shared their ideas, process the activity to validate their special needs. Tie in the pros and cons of being an athlete, in particular, to the issue of, "How does being an athlete affect your plans for the future?" Introduce the topic of sexual assault by pointing out that a "date" that goes "bad" may affect their future in ways they may never have considered. The discussion may then lead into the legal definition of rape and what the consequences may be for being accused of committing the crime.

Directions to the group:

To get us started, let's talk briefly about your experiences as athletes on this college campus. Tell me:

- What does it mean to be a male athlete at (name of school)?

- What does it mean to be a part of a team?

- How does being an athlete affect your plans for your future?

Note to facilitators: Be sure to get the men to balance the pros and cons of being an athlete and prompt them to name some of each. If the discussion is slow in getting started, share some examples of your own and ask the group whether the ideas are advantages or disadvantages. Some issues may be disadvantages for some individuals but others may argue their merit. Support any peer challenges and let the team members challenge each other. Pay attention to who the leaders in the group are, and the dynamics at work when team members are discussing the issues. If certain individuals dominate the discussion, urge others to participate.

APPENDIX B
AUDIOVISUAL TRIGGERS

- ■ Objective: To introduce the sexual assault issues in a non-threatening manner and to have prepared material for the audience to discuss

- ■ Time: 15 minutes

- ■ Materials: PSA, 1/2" VHS Playback and monitor (a large group may require a wide screen TV or two TV monitors)

Directions to facilitator:

Show one of the following public service announcements:

- *She's only Sixteen* produced by the Santa Monica Rape Treatment Center

- *Jail Cell* produced by the Santa Monica Rape Treatment Center

Process the activity by asking some of the questions below. It is typically difficult for men to talk about feelings immediately after having seen a film clip. To prompt them, you may want to ask them for just one word that describes how they are feeling . . . just one word. Then follow with some of the questions below.

Directions to the group:

- Let's talk about what you just saw. Any reactions?

- How do you feel after having watched this?

- How would you react if this had been about your sister?

- What does "no" mean?

- Does "no" always mean "no?"

- What could give a man the feeling that it is ok to have sex with a woman?

- Does submission to sexual intercourse always mean there is consent?

- If a woman got herself drunk, does she give up the right to say no?

- If a woman goes to a man's room, does she give up her right to say no?

- If a woman has a "bad" reputation, is it ok to force her to have sex?

Use these "triggers" to lead the discussion towards the following:

- Are there any circumstances under which it is OK to force a woman to have sex (i.e., she is drunk, led him on, he paid for dinner so he is owed, woman has a bad reputation, etc.)?

- Why do you think resistance is ignored? (i.e., she doesn't scream, she was giggling, she doesn't actually say no or stop, she lets a man continue after having said no, etc.)?

Note to facilitators: Frequently, rather than sharing feelings, men will make observations about what they saw (e.g., "I think the guy must have been an idiot not to stop when he heard 'no'"). Thank them for their observations and ask them to identify the feeling behind the statement (i.e., disgust, frustration, anger).

APPENDIX C
INCOMPLETE SENTENCES

■ Objective: To identify rape-supportive beliefs and to promote positive peer pressure within the group

■ Materials: pre-printed sheets with incomplete sentences, pencils

■ Time: 20 minutes

Directions to facilitator:

As the students arrive for the program, give each individual a sheet with two incomplete sentences pre-printed on each page. Tell them not to put their names on the sheet and ask them to complete the sentences individually without the help of their teammates Give them just a few minutes to complete the task. Collect the sheets after everyone is finished.

While one facilitator is leading an "icebreaker" or other activity, the other should review the sheets. Choose a few responses that are funny, thoughtful or responsible, and some that identify rape-supportive beliefs. Read the chosen responses aloud and after each response ask the group what they think. Encourage as many audience members to respond as possible to assure a variety of opinions are heard.

Suggestions are:

• "I feel someone is giving me a sexual come-on when . . . "

• "A man is owed sex when . . . "

• "I feel manipulated in a dating situation when . . . "

• "Cues from my date which make me wary are . . . "

• "When a woman sends me conflicting messages . . . where her behavior says yes and words say no, I believe . . . "

• "When beginning a relationship, I want . . . "

• "When a woman wears seductive clothes, she . . . "

Note to Facilitators: Once you have allowed the men to air their feelings about the answers, facilitators must be sure that the rape-supportive attitudes or "high risk" responses that were discussed were clearly identified as such. While it is important to let the students give their opinions, it is more important to pay close attention to apparent attitudes or stereotyped beliefs that can lead to sexual assault and to focus on them when they arise. In some instances, the men themselves may not critique or question responses that are clearly incorrect in their assumptions. The discussion can become rowdy and important educable moments can easily slip away with the distraction of many voices. The men must not leave the program believing that responses such as "a man is owed sex . . . when he pays for a date's meal" is in any way a correct or safe assumption.

APPENDIX D
AUDIOVISUAL ACTIVITIES

■ Objective: To explore the social and popular influences that contribute to a rape-prone environment

■ Time: 30-60 minutes including discussion

■ Materials: 1/2" VHS playback monitor

There are many films and videos that address rape on college campuses. Popular films with depictions of rape in them make useful trigger audio-visuals (see *Appendix E).*

Any collection of cultural media images and items such as greeting cards, magazine advertisements, posters and cartoons will help generate discussion.

Directions to facilitators:

Choose images and films that are specific to the focus of your presentation. Posters and greeting cards frequently provide images that objectify men and women. Magazine advertisements can offer images of abuse redefined as love, heterosexism, male/female gender roles and heightened sexuality for sale. A collage of images can be photographed onto slides and then organized into a logical sequence to convey the ideas you want to discuss. Or you may choose to show a video or film segment.

Mainstream films such as *Dangerous Liaisons* or *Gone With The Wind* provide images of rape that are classically promoted as seduction. *Casualties of War* and *The Accused* provide examples of gang rape. *Deliverance* or *The Rape of Richard Beck* are the most well known images of male rape. (See *Appendix E* for a complete list of films.)

Powerful images often come from survivors themselves. Television talk shows such as "Geraldo" or "The Oprah Winfrey Show" frequently broadcast segments that include survivors who describe their experiences.

The chosen segment may be short or may include several scenes. However, any film choice shouldn't run longer than 15-20 minutes.

Ahead of time, generate a list of questions specific to the film you show. Many of the current videos that address acquaintance rape on campus come with their own discussion guides. Begin by asking the group how they feel about what they saw. Help them make the connection between media images and desensitization to rape.

Facilitator's Notes: The images you choose may be powerful discussion triggers. Keep the discussion about the scenes or video focused on what happened. Some students may try to describe other scenes in the film that weren't shown to argue whether the incident depicted was truly rape. All this does is deflect the conversation. Keep it on track.

Be prepared for silence immediately following a deeply moving film segment. The audience may not be willing to discuss scenes that were clearly violent and disturbing. Lead them into discussion with techniques such as "Who can give me just one word to describe how they are feeling?" or "I found this very hard to watch. Did anyone else? What made this hard to watch?"

APPENDIX E
MAINSTREAM FILMS

Mainstream films that can be rented at local video stores or purchased from other sources offer a variety of scenes that may be used in rape education programs.

✧ *Gone with The Wind*

Rhett Butler and Scarlett O'Hara argue after Rhett has been drinking and is despondent because Scarlett has been keeping him out of her bedroom. Scarlett storms out of the dining room to go to bed. Rhett comes after her, and carries her against her will up the stairs to bed. The next scene shows Scarlett happily singing after the evening's lovemaking.

✧ *West Side Story*

Anita accidentally encounters a rival gang, the Jets, in Pop's Store. They accost her and a rape is simulated.

✧ *Extremities*

A woman is stalked by a rapist who she eventually disarms and imprisons in her home.

✧ *Casualties of War*

A soldier is pressured to participate in a gang rape of a kidnaped Vietnamese woman.

✧ *Dangerous Liaisons*

A young woman is "seduced" by an older man who is intent on introducing her to sexuality.

✧ *School Daze*

The character, Half Pint, engages in sexual intercourse as part of a fraternity initiation rite. The woman he beds is coerced and manipulated by her boyfriend, president of the fraternity, to prove her love for him.

✧ *The Accused*

Based on a true story, Jody Foster portrays a woman gang raped in a public bar while onlookers cheer the rapists on.

⬦ *The Color Purple*

A young girl is married off to an older abusive man who rapes her regularly.

⬦ *Pretty Woman*

A prostitute experiences an attempted rape by her lover's lawyer and friend. Her "knight in shining armor" stops the rape in time.

⬦ *Basic Instinct*

A frustrated policeman takes out his anger on a woman he is dating and forces her to engage in "rough sex."

⬦ *Thelma and Louise*

An attempted rape against Thelma depicts alcohol use, innocent flirtation and finally a violent self-defense response.

⬦ *Animal House*

A young fraternity man must make a decision between "having sex" with his date who is passed out from too much alcohol or acting like a "gentleman" and letting her sleep it off.

⬦ *The Program*

A football player using steroids brutally attempts an acquaintance rape of a young woman. His fellow teammates intervene.

APPENDIX F
GRAFFITI WALL

■ Objective: To allow participants a vehicle to express their feelings without having to admit ownership of them, and to confront the ideas of others

■ Time: 45 min-1 hour

■ Materials needed: Masking tape, several pieces of newsprint, magic markers for each participant

Directions to Facilitator:

Have each participant mill around and complete one or more of the following incomplete sentences on newsprint which you have previously taped onto the wall. There should be one incomplete sentence per sheet. Each participant should have his own magic marker to do so.

- Female fans who flirt with football players . . .
- Women who drink . . .
- Men who drink . . .
- Women who wear seductive clothing want to . . .
- If a woman goes back to a man's room . . .
- If a woman stays at a party/fraternity house past 2 am, she . . .
- Do guys want sex all the time? or Guys want sex . . .
- What do you hear about being a man at [name of school]?
- What do you hear about [name of school] women?
- How often do men want sex?
- How often do women want sex?
- If you don't get sex, you . . .

Bring the group back together and read some of the more interesting responses while the newsprint is still on the wall. Discuss the implications and underlying assumptions and expectations of these statements. How may these things lead to power abuse in relationships? Should they? Is there a better way to consider these issues?

(Adapted with permission of the publisher from *Acquaintance Rape and Sexual Assault Prevention Training Manual,* by Andrea Parrot, Learning Publications, Inc.: Holmes Beach, FL, 1991.)

APPENDIX G
INTERIOR DIALOGUE

■ Objective: This activity should help portray the kinds of thoughts and misunderstandings that may lead to a rape.

■ Materials needed: Two copies of the Interior Dialogue, a male and female actor/reader

■ Time: 30 minutes

Directions to the facilitators:

The male and female reader stand back to back, reading the interior dialogue from their point of view, paragraph by paragraph. This represents the difference between the male and female point of view of the same date/evening they spent together.

Directions to the students: The man and the woman before you are going to share with you their interpretations of the same events which occurred while on a date together. You will have a chance to discuss these two different points of view after they finish reading.

Discussion questions:

• Why did the male and female student have such different perceptions of the same event?

• Could those differences in perception lead to an acquaintance rape?

• How can you avoid similar misperceptions in your own relationships?

The following is part of an interior dialogue surrounding the events of a rape on a college campus.

Woman: He took me to a new ethnic restaurant I'd been dying to go to. It was really expensive but he paid for everything. We had a carafe of wine with dinner and we laughed continuously on the walk home.

Man: We had a great dinner. It was expensive, but she was worth it. She's the first girl I've met this semester who could really make me laugh. We really hit it off. She laughed at all my jokes.

Woman: We just kind of ended up at his house. That was okay because I really wanted to spend more time with him anyway. There were a number of guys hanging out in the living room. He offered me more wine, and poured each of us a glass. We sat down on the couch to talk with them, and he put his arm around me. The guys were nice but it was pretty loud, and I really wanted to talk with him alone, like we had over dinner, so I asked him if we could go someplace more quiet to talk.

Man: We went back to my apartment, and a bunch of my apartment-mates were there. I was glad they got a chance to see her. She wanted some more to drink, so I got us both some wine. After a while we got restless, and I was relieved when she asked to go someplace more quiet. As we got up to go to my room one of my friends slapped me on the butt and said, "Go for it, man!" I apologized to her for my friend's crudeness. She laughed it off, luckily.

Woman: We went up to his room, and I looked around for a place to sit down. All the chairs and most of the other horizontal surfaces were covered with books, papers and dirty laundry. Although I didn't feel comfortable, I sat on his unmade bed. I felt embarrassed about asking him to move his stuff. He sat down next to me, smiled, and kissed me. I relaxed again.

Man: As soon as we got in the room, she sat on the bed. I felt very excited. I had been waiting for this all evening. I smiled at her, and she smiled back. As I kissed her, she seemed to melt in my arms. It was apparent we both wanted the same thing. After we kissed for a while I thought we both would want some privacy so I got up and locked the door. She seemed slightly tense when I came back so I put my arms around her and kissed her to ease her back into the mood.

---

*Developed by LeeAnn Borton & Kate Rudy, Cornell University Peer Educators, 1989.

Woman: I was really enjoying kissing him, but when he got up to lock the door I began to feel uncomfortable. I thought about saying something, but decided against it because I was embarrassed and I didn't want to spoil the wonderful evening we had been having. I liked him, and I wanted him to ask me out again. When he was kissing me again and holding me so gently, I was glad that I hadn't said anything.

Man: She seemed to be enjoying herself and I could tell she really liked me. She looked great. I got very aroused kissing her and holding her close. I knew there was no turning back now. I started kissing her neck and I reached down to unbutton her shirt.

Woman: I was aroused, but I wasn't sure how far I wanted to go with him. When he started to unbutton my shirt I felt unsure but it felt nice, and I decided to let him.

Man: She seemed very receptive so I decided to unbutton and take off her pants. She protested as I unsnapped the first button, but didn't seem very serious. I felt she didn't want me to think she was too easy. I knew she would agree eventually. She was as excited as I was . . . I started to take my pants off.

Woman: He started unbuttoning my pants. I knew that I didn't want him to go that far on our first evening together. I told him to stop, but I felt bad about arousing him then stopping. We fell back while he was kissing me. He was on top of me, and I couldn't move, and I told him "no."

Man: I took her pants off after mine. She continued to protest, but I stopped listening after awhile. She had sent me all the right signals before, so it didn't seem likely that she wanted to stop now. As I entered her she started to struggle and cry. I wondered if it was her first time. As I neared orgasm she stopped struggling but continued to cry. After I pulled out I lay beside her and fell asleep.

Woman: Even though I said no he continued to pull my pants off. I couldn't stop him. I stopped worrying about what he would think and I said, "No!" loudly over and over, but he wasn't listening to me. As he forced himself into me I tried to push him off. I tried to scream but all I could do was cry. I couldn't believe he was doing this to me. After awhile I was exhausted and I stopped struggling. I just wanted it to end. I lay there feeling numb. After he was finished he rolled off of me and fell asleep. I was afraid to move. I didn't want to wake him up. I didn't want to have to see him or talk to him. Eventually I put my clothes on and walked home. I felt so dirty that I spent an hour crying in the shower.

Man: When I woke up she was gone. I wondered why she didn't say anything before she left. I had thought we had had a great time. When I called her a couple of days later, however, she hung up on me. Maybe I pushed things too far.

Woman: This is possibly the worst thing that ever happened to me. I feel empty and depressed. I can't concentrate on my work; I can't have fun. I worry about a possible pregnancy, or having to see him as I walk through campus. My friends are worried and ask me why I'm depressed, but I feel I could never tell them what has happened. I've even thought of killing myself.

APPENDIX I
SENSITIZING ACTIVITY

■ Objective: This activity is a very brief way to sensitize students to the reality of the frequency of sexual assault and rape.

■ Materials: A 3x5 card and a pencil for each participant

■ Time: 5 minutes

Description of Activity:

Each participant will write down the names of the 6 women closest to him or her. They will be asked to put the card aside for later use. The cards will not be collected, and no one will see the names they list.

After the program is over, and the participants have been exposed to the impact of rape on the victim and the dysfunction it can cause in her life (following a victim testimonial, or a reading of the pain a victim has experienced), ask them to take their cards out and look at the list. Tell them to picture the people on the cards, and ask them to consider how they would feel if one of these women confided in them that they had been victimized. Tell them that statistically 1 in 6 women will be raped or sexually assaulted during their lifetime and it could happen to one of their loved ones. Tell them that it is very likely they already know someone who has been assaulted, either as an adult, or as a child. Explain that this problem is not just a woman's issue, but everyone's issue. It is not something that happens "out there" but affects the people closest to us in our lives.

■ Objective: To sensitize the men to the trauma experienced by sexual assault victims and to increase the men's understanding of the impact on women.

■ Materials needed: Printed testimonials, video tapes with testimonials or a survivor willing to tell her story in person. If a survivor will be present, arrange ahead of time the question/answer format she would prefer . . . if at all. Some survivors prefer not to take questions from the audience. In that case, use the questions below to process.

■ Time: 30 minutes

Directions to Facilitators:

Tell the group that they will now have a chance to hear the story of a victim/survivor. Acknowledge that some of what they hear may be difficult to listen to, and assure them they will have time to process and discuss the story/video afterwards.

After the survivor's story has finished, use the following questions to trigger discussion.

Discussion questions:

- How do you feel after hearing this story?

- What did you learn from this story?

- Were you surprised by anything you heard?

- What questions do you have about the circumstances?

- What other reactions do you have?

Note to Facilitators:

These can be powerful presentations and they allow the students to vividly hear the feelings victims experience. See pages 69-70 for a more thorough discussion and guidelines for this activity.

APPENDIX K
THE ANGEL & THE DEVIL

■ Objective: To identify inappropriate and appropriate responses to rape-supportive comments about women

■ Materials: 2 chairs, 4 volunteers

■ Optional: costume props for the devil and angel, such as a pitchfork or halo.

■ Time: 20 minutes

Directions to Facilitators:

Prepare the volunteers for the role play ahead of time. Tell the volunteers that two will be sitting facing each other, and the other two are to stand behind one chair.

Each man will play one of the following roles. One will be a fellow who describes last night's date to his friend. He will tell his friend that he was with a woman who wouldn't "put out," even after having bought her drinks and even after she was dancing close with him and kissing him. The second role is the friend whose job it is to listen to what he is being told.

Each of the last two men will play a devil or angel. They will be standing behind the fellow telling the story about his date. Once the fellow has finished improvising the story, it is the devil's turn. The devil's job is to respond to the story with encouragement, graphically and crudely describing all the things the fellow should have done to get his date to have sex with him such as "So what if she resisted . . . your job is to overcome that resistance" or "be a man, she wanted it, just give her more to drink next time and get what you deserve." Then the angel's job is to contrast the devil's message and fill the fellow's ear with sensitive, caring messages such as "we must respect women" or "what if someone were talking about your sister this way."

Once the friend has heard both the devil and angel's response, his job is to come up with a message that he is comfortable saying to his friend about his comments. The entire group then joins the activity by suggesting or critiquing the friend's response.

Finish the activity with a brainstorm and make a list of the kinds of things men can say to their friends to condemn rape supportive comments.

APPENDIX L
WORKING WITH WOMEN ATHLETES

Traditionally, female sports have had to struggle to obtain and then maintain the financial, administrative and fan support generously directed at male sports. Female athletes, by the very nature of their involvement in similar activities, may share practice space, equipment and staff with male athletes.

Social interactions between men and women within an athletic department may be supportive or competitive. Because men have long dominated the sports arena, a patriarchal environment may still hold in this domain. Some sports have dramatic differences between male and female rules. Most often, it is the women's rules that ease the sport's physical requirements or contact on the field (e.g., women's lacrosse is non-contact). Because of this imbalance, women may be viewed as not "as good as" men, or not as able to withstand the physical contact needed to play the sport well. This type of attitude can exacerbate gender inequities within an athletic department. It can promote an atmosphere of inequality, where men dominate sports "properly" and women simply get in the way. This can contribute to an adversarial relationship between male and female athletes on and off the field.

Building A Healthy Environment

In contrast, respect between male and female teams may be more likely between those that share the same rigorous practices and the same game rules and regulations. Having women share workout space interrupts a gender segregated environment. Men and women who work together are more likely to develop understanding and admiration for one another, rather than an adversarial relationship.

On the other hand, women may experience sexual harassment from male athletes as a result of sharing the training space and facilities. Pats on the behind, and "hey baby" remarks from male athletes, previously reserved for women outside of the athletic world, may now happen to women who must share the previously all male athletic domain. It may be difficult for females to address this harassment if they are forced to continue to share space with their harassers. Athletic departments should be on the lookout for these types of abuses and enforce strict behavior codes that will ensure a healthy collegial environment.

Issues for Women in Athletics

Women athletes have traditionally been "exceptions to the rule." Only those who truly excelled at sports were accepted as "athletes." Otherwise, the athletic world was exclusively male. Well-known athletes like Babe Didrickson Zaharias (who excelled in many sports) and Gertrude Ederle (who swam the English Channel in 1926) were admired for their abilities, but because of their gender, were considered unusual in their athletic interests and abilities.

However, athletic opportunities for women have dramatically increased during the last few decades. In particular, the last twenty years have supported women's participation in sports, thanks to Title IX legislation.

Women athletes face particular issues as students on a campus due to interrupting historically male dominated environments. The criteria most important to athletic success have generally been defined as masculine attributes: determination, aggression, leadership, competitiveness and self-confidence (Ames, 1984). Traditionally, strong athletic women challenged what has been defined as feminine behavior and traits. Snyder & Kivlin (1975) describe how female athletes may be stereotyped by negative connotations, e.g., women who are interested in sports are unfeminine.

Stereotyping and homophobia have been the more obvious intimidations directed at women who have been athletic. Accusations of being a lesbian are common attacks hurled at women who are strong and agile because independence, competitiveness and motivation to achieve may threaten the success of heterosexual relationships (Ames, 1984). Because, traditionally, athletic prowess was not considered feminine, women whose interests led them to compete in a male-dominated athletic world had to struggle to attain public respect.

Today, some female athletes still feel "unfeminine" because of their pursuits, although it has been reported that "there is less role conflict among female college athletes who participate in sports traditionally approved for women" such as gymnastics rather than basketball (Ames, 1984). In any event, low self-esteem may lead young women to have sex with men when they want to prove that they are not lesbians. Overly feminine behaviors and fashions off the field may reflect an effort to prove they are not "one of the guys." By playing the "feminine" game, women athletes may inadvertently make themselves more vulnerable to male athletes interested in taking advantage of their insecurities.

These are just some of the issues that women athletes may face on a college campus. Educational efforts targeting just women athletes can include assertiveness training, self-defense workshops and crime prevention seminars. Programs for mixed audiences should incorporate fundamental activities that will promote h.e.r. — honesty, equality and respect.

APPENDIX M
HELPING A FRIEND WHO HAS BEEN RAPED OR SEXUALLY ASSAULTED
(A Model Brochure)

Acquaintance rape and sexual assault are a growing concern on college campuses across the nation. You may find yourself in a situation in which someone you know is raped or sexually assaulted. Would you know what to do?

This brochure exposes common myths about rape, offers specific suggestions about what to do and what not to do when someone is assaulted, and lists resources available on campus and in the Ithaca community.

We hope that as you think about the problem of acquaintance rape and sexual assault, you will want to help ensure that the Cornell community reflects the fundamental values of civilized behavior and respect for the dignity of every individual.

Cornell Advocates for Rape Education (CARE)

What's the Truth about Rape?

Believing myths won't help the victim or you. Perhaps you have heard some of these:

Myth	*Fact*
Victims are to blame in some way for the assault.	The rapist is always responsible for having committed rape. Regardless of the victim's appearance, behavior, judgment, or previous actions, the victim is not responsible for the rape. Rapists are responsible for rape.
Rape is an expression of sexual desire.	Rape is an expression of hostility and aggression with sex as the vehicle. Rape is a violent abuse of power in which one person acts without regard for the pain and trauma inflicted on another.
It won't happen to me.	One study found that one in four college women have been victims of rape or sexual assault. About 10 percent of sexual assault victims are men.
Men can't stop themselves when they are sexually aroused.	Men are capable of, and responsible for, controlling both their minds and their bodies, just as women are.
Rape is usually committed by strangers.	College women are in far greater danger of being raped by a friend or a fellow student than by a stranger. Almost 90 percent of college women who were raped knew their assailants.
It's no big deal if a woman is forced to have sex with someone she knows (for example, a friend, date, boyfriend, or spouse)—and it isn't really rape.	Sexual intercourse forced by an acquaintance is rape. In some ways it is more traumatic than stranger rape because the victim's trust in others and in her own judgment can be seriously damaged.
Men are never victims of sexual assault.	Both men and women may be perpetrators or victims of sexual assault. Unfortunately male victims rarely seek help, due to embarrassment and the fear that they will not be taken seriously.
Sexual violence does not occur between lesbians or between gay men.	Sexual violence does occur in same-sex relationships. Fear of homophobic responses may prevent victims from seeking help.
If the victim was drunk or drugged, he or she was asking for it.	Inability to give consent is not "asking for it." In New York State, forcing sexual contact on a woman or man without consent is against the law.

HOW YOU CAN HELP: DOs AND DON'Ts

Do believe your friend. People rarely lie about rape or assault.

Do listen to your friend and concentrate on understanding her or his feelings.

Do allow your friend to be silent; you don't have to talk every time he or she stops talking.

Do let your friend know that you understand her or his feelings. For example, you might say, "You must have been very frightened."

Do ask how you can help.

Do offer to accompany your friend in seeking medical attention or counseling or in going to police.

Do help your friend regain a sense of control. Support him or her in making decisions about whom to tell and how to proceed.

Do remind your friend that rape is the rapist's fault, not the victim's.

Do offer shelter or companionship so that your friend doesn't have to be alone.

Do help your friend learn about, recognize, and seek treatment for signs of rape trauma syndrome (see next page).

Don't ask questions that imply that the rape was your friend's fault, such as "Why did you go to his room?" "Why didn't you scream?" "Why didn't you run away?"

Don't touch or hug your friend unless you're sure your friend is comfortable with physical contact.

Don't act in ways that are upsetting to your friend. Be wary of phrases like "If I could find the creep, I'd kill him." Although you may be trying to be supportive, that type of comment might upset your friend even more.

Don't tell anyone about the assault without your friend's permission.

Don't tell your friend what to do; rather, help her or him explore the options. Among the complex decisions your friend will have to make are whether to report the assault to the police and whether to press charges. Rape crisis counselors and the judicial administrator can be helpful in discussing the options.

What to Do When Someone Is Raped

Immediately after a rape, you and your friend should consider taking these steps:

1. **Call the Ithaca Rape Crisis Center (277-5000).** They can provide an advocate who is knowledgeable about the needs of rape victims and who will offer to accompany you and your friend through the other two steps:

2. **Get medical attention.** Your friend will benefit from being examined for physical injury and disease and discussing options for pregnancy prevention. At this time your friend may choose to have physical and medical evidence of assault recorded for legal purposes. Should your friend decide later to press charges, such evidence will significantly increase the possibility of successful prosecution. Medical services are available at Gannett Health Center and at the Tompkins Community Hospital Emergency Room.

3. **Notify the police.** An informational report does not obligate your friend to press charges and is very helpful to police.

Rape Trauma Syndrome

Even though the actual assault is over, your friend may suffer from rape trauma syndrome, a variety of difficulties commonly experienced after a sexual assault. People respond to sexual assault in many different ways, ranging from extreme calm to extreme agitation. Your friend might experience any or all of the following reactions: emotional shock, denial, nightmares, sleeplessness, intrusive memories or thoughts about the assault, inability to work or make decisions, impaired relationships, and feelings of guilt, despair, depression, fear, anxiety, self-blame, or anger.

Some of these reactions may be short-lived; others can be troubling for months or years. In either case, it is important to know that information and help are available. Contact the Ithaca Rape Crisis Center or Gannett Health Center (Psychological Service or the sex counselor).

You Can't Do Everything

Despite your best intentions, you need to realize that there are limits to what a friend can do to help. At times your friend may not want to deal with the rape and, as a result, may even avoid you. If you need to express feelings your friend doesn't want to hear, find a trustworthy confidant or counselor. There will also be times when you need time off from helping, when you should help your friend find other support. No matter how much support you are able to give your friend, a counselor with expertise in treating victims of rape and sexual assault can play a very important role in your friend's recovery.

Important Legal Information

Forcing or coercing someone to have sexual intercourse or engage in other sexual contact is against the law. Specifically, in New York State if a woman is forced to have sexual intercourse or if she is unable to consent, the behavior of the perpetrator is considered rape. The force necessary can be any amount or threat of physical force that places the woman in fear of injury or in fear for her life. The perpetrator does not need to use a weapon or beat her to make her fearful of injury or in fear for her life.

The courts have ruled that a woman is unable to consent if she is mentally incapacitated or is physically helpless due to drug or alcohol consumption, is asleep, or is less than seventeen years of age. If a woman has intercourse without her consent, it is rape.

Forcing or coercing a man or a woman to engage in any sexual contact other than sexual intercourse under the circumstances mentioned above is considered sexual abuse or sodomy.

What We Can Do

By understanding the issues and taking action as individuals, we can begin to work toward changes that will prevent rape and sexual assault.

- Learn the facts by reading the following books:

  Against Our Will, by Susan Brownmiller

  Coping with Date Rape and Acquaintance Rape, by Andrea Parrot

  I Never Called It Rape, by Robin Warshaw

  Men on Rape, by Tim Beneke

  No Fairy Godmothers, No magic Wands: The Healing Process After Rape, by Judy H. Katz

  Recovering from Rape, by Linda Ledray

- Take a course in self-defense.

- Attend campus and community rape-awareness presentations.

- Think about and learn to recognize the connections between rape and other manifestations of inequality such as sexual harassment, racism, and violence against gays and lesbians.

- Work with others who share your concerns regarding rape and sexual assault, through community groups such as Ithaca Rape Crisis, the Ithaca Men's Network, and Planned Parenthood and campus groups such as SAFER Peer Educators, Cornell Advocates for Rape Education, the Gay, Lesbian, and Bisexual Coalition, and the Cornell Women's Center.

- Respect yourself and develop relationships based on mutual respect.

RESOURCES

For immediate assistance following a rape or a sexual assault, you can make confidential inquiries at the following places:

Ithaca Rape Crisis Center   277-5000

Department of Public Safety   255-1111

Dean of Students Office   255-6839

Gannett Health Center

   Emergencies (after hours)   255-5155

   Contraception, Gynecology, and Sexuality Service (CGSS)   255-3978

   Sex Counselor   255-6936

   Psychological Service   255-5208

Your residence hall director (RHD) or resident adviser (RA)

Other helpful resources:

Office of the Judicial Administrator   255-4680

Cornell United Religious Work   255-4214

Empathy, Assistance, and Referral Service (EARS)   255-3277

Suicide Prevention and Crisis Service of Ithaca   272-1616

Cornell University is an equal-opportunity, affirmative-action educator and employer.

APPENDIX N
RAPE AWARENESS AND
PREVENTION STRATEGIES FOR MEN

Things you can do to help you reduce your risk for rape involvement are listed below. You should always try to be aware of your surroundings and try to stay out of situations where you may force another person to do something they don't want to do.

1) Think about what you really want from or with that partner.

2) Be aware of stereotypes which prevent you from acting as you want to (such as a man not being able to say "no").

3) Feel good about yourself — and if you don't, get involved in activities and with people who will make you feel better.

4) Eliminate completely or limit any alcohol or drug consumption. Most acquaintance rapes happen when one or both partners are intoxicated or high.

5) Communicate what you really want to your partner.

6) Say what you are really thinking.

7) Set clear limits for acceptable behavior.

8) Know which behaviors constitute rape.

Most importantly:

1) Use peer pressure positively to help stop abusive behaviors which may lead to acquaintance rape (for example condemn, rather than condone the behavior of a friend who has taken advantage of a sexual partner).

2) Assume that "no" means "NO." If you are right, you have not offended your partner. If you are not, your partner will have to initiate to achieve what she/he really wants.

3) Do not exploit others sexually.

4) Don't feel as if you always have to initiate sexually, and don't initiate if you don't want to. You are allowed to feel as though you don't want to be sexually active too!

5)   Listen to the messages your partner is giving. If you are confused, ask and clarify!

6)   Understand that sexual assault and rape are crimes. An acquaintance rape happens if you have intercourse with a partner against her will and without her consent.

7)   Understand that rape is a problem for both men and women. Learn more about it and talk to your peers about ways to stop it.

Adapted from *Acquaintance Rape and Sexual Assault Prevention Training Manual* by Andrea Parrot, Ph.D., Cornell University, 1990.

APPENDIX O
BASIC RAPE EDUCATION PROGRAM
FOR STUDENT ATHLETES

Year One

- Program length: 90 minutes

- Introduction

- Time: 5 minutes

The coach, AD, or administrator introduces the program to impart the importance of the topic to be discussed.

Activity I:

- Time: 15 minutes

- Opening Discussion

- Materials Needed: PSA, 1/2" VHS Playback and monitor (A large group may require a wide screen TV or two TV monitors)

Directions to Facilitator:

Show one of the following public service announcements:

- *She's only Sixteen* Produced by the Santa Monica Rape Treatment Center

- *Jail Cell* Produced by the Santa Monica Rape Treatment Center

Directions to the group:

- Let's talk about what you just saw. Any reactions?

- How do you feel after having watched this?

- What does "no" mean?

- Does "no" always mean "no?"

- What could give a man the feeling that it is ok to have sex with a woman?

- Does submission to sexual intercourse always mean there is consent?

- If a woman got herself drunk, does she give up the right to say no?

- If a woman goes to a man's room, does she give up her right to say no?

- If a woman has a "bad" reputation, is it ok to force her to have sex?

Activity II:

■ Time: 30 minutes

■ "Internal Dialogue" *(Appendix G)*

■ Materials needed: Two copies of the "Interior Dialogue," a male and female reader.

Directions to the Facilitators:

The male and female reader stand back to back, reading the interior dialogue from their point of view, paragraph by paragraph. This represents the difference between the male and female point of view of the same date/evening they spent together.

Directions to the Students:

The man and the woman before you are going to share their interpretations of the same events which occurred while on a date together. You will have a chance to discuss these two different points of view after they finish reading.

Discussion questions:

1) Why did the male and female student have such different perceptions of the same event?

2) Could those differences in perception lead to an acquaintance rape?

3) What role did alcohol play in what happened?

4) How can you avoid similar misperceptions in your own relationships?

5) What suggestions might you have for the male and female? What are alternate ways of thinking and acting?

Activity III

■ Time: 15 minutes

■ Understanding the Law

■ Materials Needed: A handout that describes the state law as it pertains to sex offenses as well as information about the judicial processes that can be initiated on campus.

Directions to the Facilitators:

Briefly outline the fundamentals of the law as it pertains to sex crimes. Clarify any misperceptions (such as alcohol use can be used as a defense for crimes committed when intoxicated).

Activity IV:

■ Time: 5 minutes

■ What to do if it happens to someone you know

■ Materials needed: A handout that offers information about ways to respond to a victim who confides that they have been raped.

Directions to Facilitators:

Offer guidelines on how to respond to someone who may confide in the men that they have been raped or sexually assaulted.

Provide the handout as a resource they can take with them. Review the basic response preferences such as believing the person, don't threaten to kill them, don't tell them what to do but ask how you can help, etc.

Activity V:

■ Time: 10 minutes

■ Questions

Directions to Facilitators:

Leave the last few minutes for questions and discussion. Offer to stay after the program is over (so individuals can ask questions that may be more personal).

• Why Sexual Assault Prevention Programs for Athletes?

• Benefits to the individual

• Individual athletes may be prevented from committing sexual assaults

• This will save them money for an attorney, and in lost wages and tuition

- Reputation will remain untarnished

- They will avoid the emotional anguish associated with being charged with a crime

- Scholarships may be lost as a result of a sexual assault conviction

- Benefits to the team

- Team may lose a valuable member of the team if a member is charged

- Team's reputation will not be tarnished by association with an accused rapist

- Avoid negative PR

- Team spirit will not suffer as a result of a team member having been charged with rape

- Team may gain positive PR for expressing interest in an important social issue.

- Alumni may be concerned and decrease donations if member is charged

- Benefits to society

- Potential victims may remain safer

APPENDIX P
WHY SEXUAL ASSAULT PREVENTION
PROGRAMS FOR ATHLETES?

Benefits to the Individual

- Individual athletes may be prevented from committing sexual assaults

- This will save them money for an attorney, and in lost wages and tuition

- Reputation will remain untarnished

- They will avoid the emotional anguish associated with being charged with a crime

- Scholarships may be lost as a result of a sexual assault conviction

Benefits to the Team

- Team may lose a valuable member of the team if a member is charged

- Team's reputation will not be tarnished by association with an accused rapist

- Avoid negative PR

- Team spirit will not suffer as a result of a team member having been charged with rape

- Team may gain positive PR for expressing interest in an important social issue

- Alumni may be concerned and decrease donations if member is charged

Benefits to Society

- Potential victims may remain safer

APPENDIX Q
VIDEO AND
POSTER RESOURCES

The following materials were developed by and are available from Athletes for Sexual Responsibility, University of Maine, Room 15, 5749 Merrill Hall, Orono, Maine 04469-5749. Please make checks payable to the University of Maine. For more information you may call Dr. Sandra Caron at 207-581-3138.

Rape Awareness Video *(26 minutes)*

Date rape, gang rape, and the number of athletes involved in group assaults over the past year have raised questions about the exemplary status athletes hold in society. Using athletes as actors, the University of Maine has produced a videotape portraying a series of three brief vignettes. The first vignette, *The Date*, portrays a male and female whose assumptions and poor communication at the end of the date leads to acquaintance rape. In the second skit, *The Morning After*, a male involved in a gang rape at a party the night before is bragging to his friend. The friend goes along with his buddy's actions, making the erroneous assumption that the woman must have wanted or invited the assault. The final skit, *Talking with Friends*, involves two friends talking with the victim of the gang rape, but they are not supportive. They question her motives and her dress and suggest that somehow she encouraged the attack.

At critical points in each vignette, facilitators talk with the audience and generate suggestions for how the skits can be reworked to end in a positive way.

Price: $80.00

Smart Sex Video *(20 minutes)*

Everyone has heard about it: HIV, the virus which causes AIDS. It seems we are living in an age of fatal sexuality. Sex can equal death if it is unprotected. Yet how many people think it can happen to them? It can and it does. Tragically, many of those who are infected with HIV could have avoided contracting the virus if they had practiced "smart sex."

In this, their second video production, the *Athletes for Sexual Responsibility* troupe at the University of Maine has portrayed situations that deal with taking responsibility for being open and honest about our needs. With the rise in HIV infection, honesty may be the only policy. Holding back your feelings could not only damage a relationship, a career, or your self-esteem . . . your life could depend on it.

Smart Sex means more than just being able to discuss using a condom. It starts with getting in touch with all the messages . . . baggage . . . you have received about sex, how deeply you would like to be involved, and what your needs are. It means having the freedom to choose and taking responsibility for your choices.

Price: $80.00

Smart Sex Posters

Comparing smart sex to a popular sport will undoubtedly arouse the curiosity of your students. Most can't resist the temptation to step closer and find out *how* smart sex is like golf, baseball, diving or another sport.

The *Smart Sex* poster series is now available for sale. Printed posters are 11" x 17", with twenty posters per set.

Price: Set of 20 posters $40.00

APPENDIX R
BIBLIOGRAPHY

American College Health Association, 1992 April/May/June. *Action Newsletter, 30,* (3), p. 1.

Ames, N., 1984. "The Socialization of Women Into and Out of Sports." *Journal of National Association for Women Deans, Administrators & Counselors, 47,* (2), p.3-8

Berkowitz, A.D., 1994. "College Men as Perpetrators of Acquaintance Rape and Sexual Assault: A Review of Recent in: New Directions for Student Services Monograph Series," Josey Bass, San Francisco. *Research Journal of American College Health,* 1992, 40,175-181.

Berkowitz, A.D. ed. *Rape Prevention for Men: Clinical and Educational Program Strategies.* Forthcoming.

Brownmiller S., 1975. *Against Our Will: Men, Women & Rape.* Toronto: Bantam Books.

Burt, M.R., 1991. "Rape Myths and Acquaintance Rape." In: Parrot, A., Bechhoffer, L. Eds. *Acquaintance Rape: The Hidden Crime.* New York: Wiley, p. 26-40

Cornell Advocates for Rape Education, 1989. *Helping a Friend Who Has Been Raped or Sexually Assaulted.* (Available from Health Education Office, Gannett Health Center, Cornell University, Ithaca, New York 14853).

Ehrhart, J. K. & Sandler, B.R., 1985. *Campus Gang Rape: Party Games?* Washington, DC: Association of American Colleges.

Elgin, S.H., 1993. *Genderspeak: Men, Women, and the Gentle Art of Verbal Self-defense.* Wiley & Sons: New York.

Eskenazi, G., 1990, June 3. "Athletic Aggression and Sexual Assault." *New York Times,* Section 8, p.1,4.

Eskenazi G., 1991, February. "Male Athletes and Sexual Assault." *Cosmopolitan,* pp. 220-223.

Finkelhor, D., Hotaling, G., Lewis, I.A. & Smith, C., 1990. "Sexual Abuse in a National Survey or Adult Men and Women: Prevalence, Characteristics and Risk Factors." *Child Abuse & Neglect,* 14, pp. 385-401.

Goodchilds, J.D., Zellman, G.L., Johnson, P.B. & Giarruso, R., 1988. "Adolescents and Their Perceptions of Sexual Interactions." In A.W. Burgess (Ed.), *Rape and Sexual Assault II,* (pp. 245-270) New York: Garland.

Heasley, R. & Barker, J., 1994, March. *The Dialectic of Sexuality: Rethinking the Polarized Gendering Paradigm.* Paper presented at the Eastern Sociological Association Conference, Baltimore, MD.

Hoffman, R., 1986, March 17. "Rape and the College Athlete: Part One." *Philadelphia Daily News,* p. 104.

Janis, I.L., 1972. *Victims of Groupthink,* Boston: Houghton-Mifflin.

Johnson, C., 1991, October 7. "When sex is the issue." *U.S. News & World Report,* p. 34-36.

Kohlberg L. & Kramer R., 1969. "Continuities and Discontinuities in Childhood and Adult Development." *Human Development,* 12, 93-120.

Koss, M.P., Gidycz, C.A., & Wisniewski, N., 1987. "The Scope of Rape: Incidence and Prevalence of Sexual Aggression and Victimization in a National Sample of Higher Education Students." *Journal of Consulting and Clinical Psychology,* 55, (2), 162-170.

Lenihan, G.O., Rawlins, M.E., Eberly, C.G., Buckley, B. & Masters, B., 1992. "Gender Differences in Rape Supportive Attitudes Before and After a Date Rape Education Intervention." *Journal of College Student Development,* 33, 331-338.

Lundberg-Love, P. & Geffner, R., 1989. "Date Rape: Prevalence, Risk Factors and a Proposed Model." In: Pirog-Good, M.A., & Stets, J.E. *Violence in Dating Relationships: Emerging Social Issues.* New York: Praeger, Chapter 9.

Jack, M., 1992, January. "Seven Years Ago I Raped a Woman." *Glamour* magazine, pp. 11, 144-145.

Malamuth N., 1981. "Rape Proclivity Among Males." *Journal of Social Issues,* 37 138-157.

Marchell, T., Hofher, J., Parrot, A., & Cummings, N., 1992, November. "Prevention by education." *Athletic Management,* 44-48.

Miedzian, M., 1991. *Boys will Be Boys: Breaking the Link Between Masculinity and Violence.* Doubleday: New York.

Mosher, D.L. & Anderson, R. D., 1986. "Macho Personality, Sexual Aggression and Reactions to Guided Imagery of Realistic Rape." *Journal of Research in Personality,* 20 (1), 77-94.

Muehlenhard CL., 1990. "Male's Heterosocial Skill and Attitudes Towards Women as Predictors of Verbal Sexual Coercion and Forcible Rape." *Sex Roles.* 23, 241-259.

Neimark J., 1991, May. "Out of bounds? The Truth About Athletes and Rape." *Mademoiselle*, pp. 196-199, 244-245.

Nelson, M.B. 1991, June 22. "Bad Sport." *New York Times*, p. A21.

O'Sullivan, C., 1991. "Acquaintance Gang Rape on Campus." In Parrot, A. & Bechhofer, L. (Eds), *Acquaintance Rape: The Hidden Crime* (pp.140-156). New York: John Wiley & Sons.

Parrot, A. & Bechhofer, L. (Eds.). (1991). *Acquaintance Rape: The Hidden Crime*. John Wiley & Sons: New York.

Parrot, A. (1993). Coping with Date Rape and Acquaintance Rape. New York: Rosen.

Parrot, A., Cummings, N., Marchell, T., & Hofher, J. (1994). "A Rape Awareness and Prevention Model for Male Athletes." *Journal of American College Health,* 42 (4), January.

Perry W., 1970. *Forms of Intellectual and Ethical Development in the College Years*. New York: Holt, Reinhart & Winston.

Sanday, P., 1990. *Fraternity Gang Rape*. New York: NYU Press.

Sanday, P., 1981. "The Socio-cultural Context of Rape: A Cross Cultural Study." *Journal of Social Issues,* 37, (4), 5-27.

Schaeffer, A.M., & Nelson, E.S., 1993. "Rape-Supportive Attitudes: Effects of On-Campus Residence and Education." *Journal of College of Student Development,* 34, 175-179.

Snyder, E.E. & Kivlin, J.E., 1975. "Women athletes and aspects of psychological well-being and body image." *Research Quarterly,* 46, (2), 191-199.

Spence, J.T. & Helmrich, R., 1972. "The attitudes towards women scale: An objective instrument to measure attitudes toward the rights and roles of women in contemporary society." J.S.A.S. Catalog of Selected Documents in *Psychology,* 2, 1-48.

Staff., 1990, August 6. "Sex and the Sporting Life," *Time* magazine, pp.76-77.

Warshaw, R., 1988. *I Never Called It Rape*. New York: Harper & Row.

NOTES

NOTES

NOTES

NOTES

NOTES

NOTES